CALLED TO BUSINESS

CALLED
TO
BUSINESS

PURSUING ECONOMIC

SUCCESS WITH

SPIRITUAL PURPOSE

RANDY STEVENSON

iUniverse, Inc.
Bloomington

Called to Business
Pursuing Economic Success with Spiritual Purpose

NIV - Scripture is taken from *The Holy Bible, New International Version*. Copyright 1973, 1978, 1984 International Bible Society. Used by permission of Zondervan Bible Publishers.

AMP / KJV - Scripture is taken from *The Amplified Bible*. Copyright 1954, 1958, 1962, 1964, 1965, 1987 by The Lockman Foundation. All rights reserved. Used by permission. (www.Lockman.org)

NASB - Scripture is taken from the *New American Standard Bible*. Copyright 1960, 1962, 1963, 1968, 1971, 1973, 1975, 1977 by the Lockman Foundation. Used by permission.

NKJV - Scripture is taken from the *New King James Version*. Copyright 1982 by Thomas Nelson, Inc. Used by permission. All rights reserved.

iUniverse books may be ordered through booksellers or by contacting:

iUniverse
1663 Liberty Drive
Bloomington, IN 47403
www.iuniverse.com
1-800-Authors (1-800-288-4677)

Because of the dynamic nature of the Internet, any web addresses or links contained in this book may have changed since publication and may no longer be valid. The views expressed in this work are solely those of the author and do not necessarily reflect the views of the publisher, and the publisher hereby disclaims any responsibility for them.

Any people depicted in stock imagery provided by Thinkstock are models, and such images are being used for illustrative purposes only.
Certain stock imagery © Thinkstock.

ISBN: 978-1-4759-8043-1 (sc)
ISBN: 978-1-4759-8044-8 (e)

Printed in the United States of America

iUniverse rev. date: 6/11/2013

For Shannon,

the beautiful woman who took a chance on a new Christian
more than three decades ago. Not only have you endured being
the wife of an entrepreneur, but you have been a wonderful
life partner and an awesome mother to our children. It has
been exciting to experience our spiritual walk together.

And for Charlotte Hale Pindar,

who has been my friend, editor, and encourager. Without you, I doubt
this project would have ever been completed. I know that I am only
one of many that you have blessed with your skills and friendship!

But seek first His kingdom and His righteousness, and all these things will be given to you as well.

—Matthew 6:33 (NIV)

CONTENTS

INTRODUCTION

alled to Business could be described as a motivational manual. It was written to encourage Christian businesspeople to pursue the dreams God has placed into their hearts, while offering practical business and spiritual guidance to the issues that are unique to them. As businesspeople, we find our work challenging, exciting, and invigorating, but often we struggle to connect our drive and passion for our work with our spirituality.

Initially, I thought this struggle was one that only I dealt with. I did not attend church as a child, but became a Christian at the age of twenty-five. By then I had completed a tour of duty in the army, finished a degree in business and finance, and planned to begin working toward a graduate degree in business. I had already owned two small businesses by that young age and was now ready to pursue the great American dream of becoming successful and wealthy! However, when I became a Christian, my priorities changed. I began to do things "God's way" as I desired to fully serve Him. But … I still loved business. I was still very committed to the success of my work. *Is my desire to be successful wrong?* I would often ask myself.

The proper question to be asked of me as well as others who pursue success must be "Why?" Why do we want to be successful? For some, money is the answer. For others, the reason may be pride, power, or a fear of failure; however, we may find that our drive for success actually may be fueled by God. *Called to Business* discusses the fact that God has a plan and a purpose for each one of us. He has a part for each of us to play in the expansion of His kingdom through the spreading of the gospel.

By sharing personal experiences from my forty-year business career, real-life examples of Christian businesspeople, and relevant principles from scripture, I have attempted to address this inner·struggle to connect our passion for business with our passion for Him. This·book will cause you, the reader, to rethink the three spiritual issues that challenge so many Christian businesspeople: *purpose, leadership, and success.* This book will hopefully enable you to become totally free in your spirit to pursue great business and economic success, empowered by a great spiritual purpose!

Purpose:

Called to Business immediately begins addressing the ever-so-critical issue of life purpose in the first chapter. We address the questions that every Christian businessperson must face:

- Why do I chase after sales, develop budgets, and set goals and quotas week after week?
- Am I serving God in my work or am I simply serving myself?
- Might my business/company have a spiritual purpose over and above meeting the needs of my customers?

You will read and observe the answers I found to these very questions that challenge so many Christian businesspeople today, just as they challenged Solomon in his day. We will discuss how we can blend our business careers into our spiritual work and purpose.

Leadership:

A Christian leader's greatest challenge can come in the daily fast-paced, decision-making life at the workplace. Such daily challenges will also present the greatest opportunities for Christians to display the character and benefit of a relationship with the Lord. *Called to Business* will address questions such as:

- Does a Christian business leader lead differently than others? If so, how?
- What principles should act as a rudder to guide a Christian leader through the intense and often treacherous waters of the business world?
- How do our actions in the workplace affect others, spiritually speaking?

You will find examples and principles that will not only propel you to greater success in the business world, but also to greater success as a leader for Christ.

<u>Success:</u>

Success in the workplace is to be measured by the footprint we leave upon the earth, the impact we have on lives. Our positions and money are to be used to influence those around us for the betterment of humanity. We are to be expanders of the kingdom of God—His vessels and His foot soldiers on this earth. As you read this book, it is my hope that you will find answers to questions such as:

- How does God define success?
- Is financial gain a result of excellence and success?
- What responsibilities come with my financial success?

Displacing many of the misinterpretations of scripture regarding money and success, I hope to help liberate the financially successful from feelings of guilt and condemnation. I will also address the responsibility we have in stewarding financial resources. You may be surprised to find that the business and financial successes of Christians have a very important purpose in God's plan for His kingdom!

It is my hope that reading *Called to Business* will help you operate your businesses more successfully by utilizing God's principles of business, leadership, and finance. The concept that God places individuals into business for Kingdom purposes is new to many, but true. **Economic success with spiritual purpose** can be a life-changing experience for individuals, companies, and those that need to see and hear the gospel of Christ.

Your business and spiritual mission, however large or small in the eyes of the world, is yours to complete. We should be able to stand before a mirror daily and ask ourselves, "Am I pursuing success and purpose with all that God has given me?" And in the end, we should be able to stand before the Lord and hear the words, "Well done, good and faithful servant."

SECTION ONE

PURPOSE

Therefore, if anyone is in Christ, he is a new creation;
the old has gone, the new is come!
—2 Corinthians 5:17 (NIV)

Chapter One

"My" Business: A Kingdom of Self-Protection

"Let me out," I said as my wife slowed the car on an interstate exit ramp. "I want to walk the rest of the way home."

Shannon immediately pulled over, and I got out of the vehicle, intending to walk the remaining mile or so alone. Rain was falling, and as I walked I began to weep. Never before in my life had I felt so completely worthless.

At first my turmoil seemed to be business related. Everything I had attempted during the past year either nose-dived or never got off the ground, and I simply could not understand it, for I had always operated small businesses easily and successfully. Even as a college student, I had owned and operated a couple of small businesses that helped pay my way through school.

Business savvy seemed to be part of my DNA, and I thrived on it. For me, business was a stimulating chess game I could easily win … and I was not used to failure. Furthermore, I always had thought my success in the business world pretty much defined me as a person. I felt that the lack of success in that primary role defined me as a failure in my career as well as as a man, a husband, and a father. Failure was unacceptable.

If I achieved business success, however, I believed that would define me as someone who was successful in life. It would mean that my wife, my family, and the rest of the world would view me as a person of substance and value, right? But that day, as I trudged along the muddy roadside with rain and tears streaming down my face, I felt totally worthless … lower than the dirt beneath my shoes. I had begun to see the truth. I did not know my life or myself as God did. I had begun to realize that my "success" meant little in God's evaluation of me. Nor did even my best work have much effect on my worth as a husband or a dad.

As I absorbed those truths, I began to realize how heavy the burden of constantly trying to prove myself to those I loved, and to myself, had become. I had tried to prove my worth by meeting the world's standards of success instead of God's, and I had withheld this part of my life from Him in thinking I could be successful on my own. Now, finally, I was broken in spirit. I was ready to give everything to God, including my business aspirations. What a fool I had been years before when, as a new Christian, I promised God that He could have "everything except my career and my business." I wanted to make it big, I said, and then He could have that too.

These inner transactions took only a few minutes. Glancing around, I realized that my sweet wife had not driven home but had followed me in the car. She pulled up alongside me, I got back into the car, and together Shannon and I went home. I felt emptied of years of conflict and filled with an enormous new peace.

Self-Protection

During the next days, weeks, and months I experienced an amazing transition. I continued to see that as a means of self-protection, I had not allowed God to control my business and career. I had allowed my business success to define me as an individual to others and myself.

According to a *Wall Street Journal* editorial, psychologists have been telling us for years how unhealthy it is to base our self-worth on job performance. Yet a majority of Americans state they derive their sense of identity from their jobs.

Most satisfied workers can agree with that statement to some extent. We feel our jobs somehow complete us, but it was even more than that for me. In my case, I was insecure and I needed to prove myself to the world and those around me. Therefore, I could not allow God into this area of my life. It was my kingdom, my territory ... mine to build and protect. After all, God might have had plans for me that conflicted with the business success I craved and needed so I could feel good about myself.

That same rainy night, I decided that rather than build my kingdom of personal success, my fortress of protection, self-worth, and value, I would begin to work on building God's temple. Now utterly repulsed by the idea that I had placed my own ambitions ahead of the business of God, I found myself willing to go to the other extreme. I would abandon business, if necessary, and give myself to foreign missions instead. Or I could simply take a job somewhere, if God wanted me to. In short, I would do whatever God wanted me to do. The idea that He actually might have programmed and intended for me to succeed in the business world never once entered my head.

Others describe similar transactions with God. The total surrender and the willingness to go anywhere, do anything, and follow Him at all costs definitely becomes the costliest yet most rewarding "business decision" we ever make. The paradigm shift is huge, and at times it can seem almost impossibly difficult. But once the decision is made, God begins to restore a man or woman in every way. In my quiet times each day, I began listening for and hearing the voice of God for both my business and personal life as I opened up to His will. As I committed more fully to building His kingdom rather than my own, He began restoring me rapidly and completely. He set my feet on solid rock instead of the slippery sands of that rain-soaked roadside where I had surrendered everything to Him.

NEW PROSPERITY

During the next few months of day-by-day discoveries, God allowed me to see and learn about His purposes for the world's businesses and their place in kingdom work. He began restoring the prosperity I had known, and He began to restore my sense of self-worth. He began to heal me of my hidden insecurities, my fears of failure, and the need to build my kingdom of self-protection. Most significantly, God began teaching me about the importance and high calling of business in His work. Gradually these truths took root in my life:

- My love and appreciation of business is a God-instilled trait.
- God can and will use believers in the business world. We are as important to the kingdom as pastors and preachers.
- As He expands our territories, He can use us to further expand His kingdom.
- He wants us to prosper ... after all, we are His children.

MISCONCEPTIONS AND TRUTHS

Serious Christians often become extremely ambivalent about various forms of business success. I certainly am not the first man or woman to experience the kind of anguished soul-searching that leads to becoming totally broken and yielding to God.

When we are at this point, we often ask ourselves:

- Should I turn my back on the business world and become a pastor? (This can lead to some pretty unhappy, even mediocre, church leaders.)
- Is it wrong or unholy for me and my business to prosper financially?
- Does a pastor/preacher/evangelist hold a lofty position in God's eyes, while a Christian banker, teacher, or business owner falls far short?
- Does God have some sort of rating scale for various careers, callings, businesses, and professions?

The answers to such questions about our lives can be found, of course, in the Holy Bible. For someone like me, fascinated and enthused by business, my work and career seem almost like a sport. Business is a game of strategy, and I enjoy playing and winning the game. The Bible, I found, actually teaches that it is okay for me to enjoy business and to be happy with success. It was my perspective that needed to change … not my gifting.

Furthermore, I learned that the desire to win and to succeed is not wrong. God created us to become builders. He programmed us for success, not failure. God creates and builds, and He designed us after Himself. According to Genesis 1, God

- created the world and everything in it,
- gave humanity dominion over all creation,
- initiated the establishment of His kingdom on this earth, and
- placed humanity here to continue the process.

As children of God, we have inherited His traits. We love to create, build, and expand … just as He does.

KINGS AND PRIESTS

Revelation 5:10 states that we, the body of Christ, are kings and priests. This song of the angels also says that we are to reign on the earth. This scripture is paralleled in the Old Testament by Exodus 19:6, where God called Moses to Him and instructed him to tell the Israelites, "you will be for me a kingdom of priests and a holy nation."

From Adam to Moses to the angels of Revelation, the Bible makes clear that God has placed His people here to exhibit leadership on the earth. Furthermore, we are to be both spiritual leaders and earthly leaders … kings and priests.

Priests are spiritual leaders.

Kings are earthly leaders.

Jesus Christ is our king. He is also our high priest.

In Jesus, we are able to see a man having both dominion over the physical earth and authority over the spiritual realm. He empowered us, the body of Christ, with the same dominion and authority. He actually instructs us to do even greater things on this earth than He did (John 14:12).

In his book *Kings and Priests*,[i] David High described how he wrestled with a major change in his life. After High had been a pastor for many years, God suddenly moved him out of the ministry and into the business world. For years after that, he felt displaced and considered himself a second-class Christian. After all, he had been demoted, had he not?

The Lord then took High to the Old Testament and began to reveal the importance of priests *and* kings. Both were leaders, he saw, with equally important roles.

Priests were ministers. They ministered to the Lord and to the people. They heard God, gave counsel to the king, and were responsible for the temple.

Kings ran the government. They were responsible for their country's economy, protection, and overall welfare. A good king kept his kingdom strong.

The priest gave counsel to the king. He told the king what the Lord was saying regarding the situation at hand; he gave the king the word of the Lord. Read about King David, and you easily find evidence of his relationship with the priests. While the king held ultimate earthly authority in the land, he never told the priest what to do. The priest was able to advise the king and tell him what to do, but only because the king *allowed* him to be in such a position.

Priest	King
Hears God	Deals with people
Cares for the temple	Runs the economy
Gives direction	Takes action
Empowers the king	Places the priest in position willingly
Leader—called of God	Leader—called of God

We can see how the king and the priest work together. One is not complete without the other. Each strengthens the other and strengthens the kingdom by working with the other.

As Christians, we are called to be both kings and priests. We are to have the ability to hear God and the willingness to act upon His instructions. We have both the spiritual strengths and abilities of the priests and the earthly dominion of the king. We are uniquely empowered by God to act as both.

BALANCE

As we work in the business world eight, ten, or twelve hours per day, we are functioning primarily as a king. We are dealing with the physical realm of the earth. However, if we tune in our spiritual ears, *the priestly side* of our being, we also are able to "hear" directly from the Lord to know and understand what we are to do in a given situation. We can position our kingly self under our priestly self in order to hear God, just as the Old Testament king would position himself below the priest for the same purpose. Our king (business) side must then be willing to submit to the voice of the priest (godly) side and act accordingly in our business.

As businesspeople we can choose not to listen and submit to God and His instructions, just as David could have chosen not to listen to Nathan the priest. He did listen, however, even when it hurt. He listened and obeyed; he wanted to hear God's instructions. David was one of the few kings of the Old Testament who conducted his kingship in this manner until his death.

Though extremely successful, David made mistakes just as we do. Some of these were costly and often simply were human sin. However, King David would always allow the Lord to rebuke him and bring correction. David realized most of his problems occurred when he acted out of his human judgment or selfishness rather than seeking God's input in a situation. He always acknowledged his sins and accepted the consequences of his mistakes because he desired to do the will of God. That was the secret of his success.

WARFARE

As we work in the business world, we function primarily on *the kingly side* of our being. We, like kings, are involved in the economy. We have projects; we must deal with threatening situations; and we must make decisions that will have consequences. Like David, we need to have our "priestly" ears open so that we can hear God's will in every situation.

We must realize that we, like the kings of the Old Testament, are on a battlefield. While the business world may be our battlefield, the battles are spiritual. In fact, the Bible tells us that our warfare is not against flesh and blood, but against spiritual forces of evil (Ephesians 6:12). This means that while there is a physical business world in which we must survive, as Christians we are given spiritual responsibilities and, therefore, spiritual battles as well. Satan does not want us to win, for we are fighting on the side of God, who is Satan's enemy. We must be a tough, salty army, as we do often find ourselves on the front lines of spiritual battles.

This concept is good for those who work full time in the ministry. Pastors and others in full-time ministry operate primarily out of the priestly side of their being, but they also need to be able to act upon God's strategic instructions just as a "king" would. If a minister ignores the kingly (administrative leadership) side, he or she may not have the stewardship principles and practices needed for the ministry. This often happens, and it is why we may find ministries in financial trouble, not properly organized, or with frustrated employees.

Just as Jesus was, we are to be both in one: kings and priests.

ASK YOURSELF

So we ask ourselves, "Does my work in the business arena really constitute ministry?" As Jesus often did, we can answer this question with a question: "Was King David in ministry?"

The answer is yes, King David was in the ministry, just as Nathan the prophet was. They both were used by God to further establish His kingdom. Both were called; both were needed. They had separate anointings (consecrations), which were equally important. As was discussed earlier, these two types of leadership worked together in order to fulfill God's purpose and will.

As businesspeople, we need to raise up the priest within us when we are on the job in the marketplace. Instead of allowing Satan to cause us to feel like second-class Christians, we must realize that we hold a very important and strategic place of leadership in God's kingdom. We must realize that our business career is not separate from our spiritual walk; they should be as one. Our business life and spiritual life must be merged and cannot remain separated if we are to fulfill God's desire for us.

Examine yourself:

— Is my business or profession the ministry to which I have been called?
— Do I listen for God's direction in my business?
— Am I willing to follow His advice and lead … even when I do not understand the full picture?

And the most important business question of all follows:

— Have I mentally deeded my business office, property, cash flow, and all other holdings to God? If so, is He my CEO? Am I listening to His instructions rather than to my will?

As we recognize that our desks may be our pulpits—our opportunity to influence the world for Christ—we can begin to understand the nature of true success. I encourage you to determine which kingdom you choose to build: your temporary kingdom of worldly success or the kingdom of God with its lasting eternal value.

CHAPTER TWO

GOD WORKS AND SO DO I

Work, I always thought, was something we did to provide food, shelter, and other necessities of life for our families and ourselves. This was a fact of life with which I was raised. On the spiritual side, I, like many other Christians, was taught that work was a curse caused by the fall of Adam.

The Bible teaches us that when Adam and Eve sinned, they were cast out of the Garden of Eden. God told Adam that only by the sweat of his brow and by painful toil would he be able to obtain food (Genesis 3:17–18). Adam and all men must now labor for sustenance as a result of his mistake.

Man adapted to that curse and principle. Today's economic system pretty much hinges upon the fact that unless we work, we do not have what we need or want. Our culture also teaches us that our work is a measurement of our value to society. Most of us grew up hoping and expecting our work or profession would be important and exciting. "What do you want to be when you grow up? A fireman, a police officer ...?" This is a question we heard as children from the time we began to talk with our parents and teachers. However, once we reach adulthood many of us become frustrated because our work is not fulfilling, and we find that work becomes a demanding and even enslaving factor in our life, little more than a means of sustenance.

A careful study of the Bible, however, reveals that work was not designed to provide food and shelter for families. Work actually began in the Garden of Eden with Adam, who tended the garden, named the animals, and was instructed to assume dominion over the entire earth. Adam's work had nothing to do with his sustenance, but was focused on his contribution to the earth. Jesus and Paul also address this very issue by instructing us not to worry about our sustenance, but to work so that we may give to others (Matthew 6:25; Ephesians 4:28).

Rather than ask our children what they want to be when they grow up, perhaps we should ask them what they think God wants them to do with their life. What would happen if we taught our children that their occupation should be focused upon their "contribution" to the kingdom rather than their means of "taking" a living?

ONE WOMAN'S BUSINESS

In 1979 Jackie Beavers, an Atlanta housewife who was divorced and rearing two young sons, entered the business world. Jackie had not one iota of business knowledge or experience, but she had a thorough knowledge of the Bible. Nearly destitute and beset with fears, she had nowhere to turn for help except God.

Then a friend gave her a forty-dollar start-up kit that enabled Jackie to distribute skin care products. She was in business and soon brought other women into the company to work with her. But how would she train these people? How would she train herself?

In her book *Pour for More: Receiving God's Grace*, she describes what happened after her desperate prayer for guidance. "In my spirit I heard God say, 'Jackie, if you will stick to my word for training material, I will keep your manna fresh.'"

Within days Gary O'Malley, vice president of a motivational training company, knocked on her door. At the heart of his presentation were five questions:

- Who is God?
- Who am I?
- Why do I exist?
- How should I live?
- What would God have me do?

"Gary helped me and the women who worked with me determine our unique purpose in God, and from that moment until this day, I have never used anything but God's word (Bible) for training," she wrote. Imagine the impact this has had on her *employees*. Imagine the impact this has had on her *customers*.

Within six months, Jackie Beavers had several hundred women working with her and selling hundreds of thousands of dollars' worth of product. "We were selling a good product, having fun doing it, and prayerfully following God's lead with every step we took. We were operating out of a vision, and God was blessing us mightily," she said.

Her group generated so much business that Jackie's commissions skyrocketed. When the company offered her a then impressive $50,000 per year salary, she accepted it. God had met her need for financial security. Beyond that, however, God led Jackie through the basic business training she would need later when she established her own new company. He also helped her hone her speaking and business training skills. She has become an author, platform speaker, and much sought-after Bible teacher.

The businessperson, even a complete novice, who turns to God in his or her need will surely prosper. Jackie Beavers is just one among countless others who speak eloquently about how God works in us and through us as we work with and for Him. That principle, the essence of marketplace ministry, attracts more and more businesspeople today. Evangelist Billy Graham is quoted as calling marketplace ministry "Christianity's next thrust."

To place one's talents, skills, business, career, profession, and future into the hands of God may seem ridiculously radical, even naïve, to some. Those who try it, however, experience peace, prosperity, and life purpose they otherwise could never find.

Your competitive or even aggressive business talents and skill, used for the purposes of God's kingdom, could become more far-reaching than you can possibly imagine. To decide to trade mundane daily business efforts and hopes of career and financial success for God's purposes in the business world presents the most profoundly important business decision any career-minded person can make.

Our God Works

The desire in us to work is natural—given to us by our Creator. And just as we work, so does God. God Himself is our example.

Genesis 1 tells us that in the very beginning of this earth as we know it, God worked for six days creating our world and all that is in it. He then rested for one day. God continued to develop the world and His people as history unfolded, providing and caring for them, whatever their actions and state of obedience to Him.

God continues to work today as well … in both the spiritual realm and the natural realm. Omnipresent and omnipotent—present everywhere, all-knowing, and all-powerful—He rules over everything, yet comes to us in our hearts, our lives, and our daily affairs.

Why Does God Work?

What is God's purpose for His activity in our world? The Bible tells us He works to expand His kingdom on this earth so all may know Him and come into fellowship with Him, now and in eternity.

God puts world leaders in place, and He gives us wisdom and creative abilities for new thoughts and innovations, yet He takes time to hear and directly answer our individual prayers. His Holy Spirit remains present and at work in every believer.

The magnificent, ongoing works of our Almighty God are far-reaching, personal, timely, and eternal, and they continue in our lives and far beyond. God works for the lasting good of all He has created. Most remarkably, we have been called and anointed to work beside Him for His highest purposes.

WHY YOU AND I WORK

Like God, you and I desire to work. Created in His image, we have innate desires to create, construct, order, and rule. Yet these gifts and desires were not instilled in us for the purpose of self-provision and preservation, but for the expansion of His goodness and kingdom.

Both Jesus and the apostle Paul instructed us not to worry about what we would eat or what we would wear, but to "seek first His kingdom and His righteousness." Put God's purposes first, Jesus promised, and "all these things will be added to you" (Matthew 6:33, NASB).

It is not hard to understand and acknowledge these instructions as spiritual truth. It is much harder, though, to get a handle on the power of working together with the God of the universe, using and growing in the talents He has placed within us.

DAILY NEEDS

Our working life usually is driven by our perceived "daily needs"—car payments, school supplies, tuition payments, and dozens of other ongoing obligations our work is supposed to supply. As was mentioned in the previous section, scripture says, "All these things, Jesus said, will be given to us if we first seek His kingdom and His righteousness" (Matthew 6:33, NASB).

That is a huge promise. Men and women who believe it and choose to accept it—those who see their life, their work, and their calling from God's perspective—do not *worry* about how they will fund house payments, new appliances, or braces for someone's teeth. Again and again, they see God faithfully provide for their every need. He is the author of "every good and perfect gift" (James 1:17, NIV). But the opposite idea, that we meet our needs and our family's needs through our work—leaving God out of the equation—is exactly what most working people do. I have found that when I take matters into my own hands, then the provision needed in my life is dependent upon and limited to my performance. I have learned that God will come through for me and provide answers and financial solutions even when I cannot foresee a good outcome. If we only could learn to believe the scriptures and trust Him, we would not need to waste time worrying.

However, God does intend for us to work as He works. He continually works to expand His kingdom on the earth so all may come to know His love, His grace, and His mercy. All of His creation is to know Him and accept His leadership. As Christians we are to be industrious in the workplace but committed to carrying the gospel to the uttermost parts of the earth, to every tribe and nation.

It is hard to understand why God has chosen you and me as His coworkers. Throughout history, however, God has used ordinary people to accomplish great things of eternal value.

BUSINESSPEOPLE IN KINGDOM WORK

As businesspeople, we have an important role in carrying out Jesus's Great Commission. We must recognize, however, that we cannot build two kingdoms at once. We can build our own kingdom of sustenance and self-preservation, or we can do our part to build the kingdom of God.

Our calling to the business arena enables us to participate in important kingdom-building efforts. Successful businessmen have conceived some far-reaching plans. Thousands of homes for low-income families are built worldwide through Habitat for Humanity; orphaned children are cared for by Parental Care Ministries; and medical assistance is provided worldwide through Physicians Aiding Physicians Abroad.

The list could fill this book. An Atlanta businesswoman travels to Armenia to teach women with centuries-old knitting skills how to restore a knitting factory, revive ancient patterns, and learn to establish a co-op and market their products.

Other businesses establish food banks, clinics, and college scholarship funds, or they distribute goods and clothing to the homeless and others in need. Often projects such as collecting used wheelchairs, walkers, and hospital beds to give to low-income patients begin locally and become a model for other states and nations.

PARENTAL CARE MINISTRIES

My good friend and next-door neighbor is a pediatrician. Our wives are friends as well and pray together often, as do "Bub" and I. He and I also were in a weekly men's prayer group for several years.

While Bub loved children and taking care of their medical needs, it was apparent to him and all of us who prayed with him that he felt something was missing in his life. He even began to question if his purpose in life was really to help sick children every day, because it wasn't bringing the fulfillment he had anticipated, even though he was highly respected and very successful. He began offering more prayer time to his patients and their families, and, although this did bring increased focus and purpose to his work as a doctor to children, he still felt that something was missing.

A few short years ago, his wife, Monica, traveled to Africa with a church group as a part of a missions program. While on the mission trip, she met a pastor from Uganda who was housing and trying to educate about 150 orphans. These orphans were just a few of the thousands of children who had lost their parents to the AIDS epidemic. That meeting with Pastor Emmy impacted Monica so much that she and Bub immediately planned a trip to Uganda to see if they could be of help. As a result of their heart-touching visit, they founded Parental Care Ministries.

Yes, Bub and Monica now knew what their life work was to be. Bub's passion was ignited there in Africa, and he let that fire motivate him to birth a ministry, figure out a budget, and raise the money through an "adopt-a-child" program. Today, Parental Care Ministries has six campuses where they educate, feed, love, and care for over one thousand orphans and children of peasants. They recently purchased a farm that is self-sustaining in order to provide vocational training to these children.

Dr. Mark Barret (Bub) does not practice medicine within the ministry ... he practices the powerful love of God by using the gifts and talents he has been given. His position and influence within his profession and community have allowed him to elevate the ministry to a level he never dreamed of. He has found that he and his wife are excellent visionaries, leaders, and managers ... using skills not fully tapped into within his medical practice. Yet it has been his medical practice —his vocation—that has allowed him the opportunity to pursue his true life work—his spiritual calling. He also has a new name. The children of Uganda call him "Epa," and you can find out why in a book about them, *So Much More: The Story of Parental Care Ministries,* by Patrick Butler.

A PASSION FOR BUSINESS

The business world and professional world is where we can express our God-given instincts for working and building. When this leads to solid or even spectacular success, the world often criticizes Christian businesspeople, assuming their motives are money, greed, or pride. In a few cases that may be true, but most enter the business world because they enjoy it, pure and simple.

During the two decades when I owned a commercial flight school, I observed thousands of pilots who had a passion for aviation. I enjoyed flying, but I never trained for a license. For me, aviation was a business, not a hobby or dream. But pilots of every age, I noticed, were in love with the very thought of flying. In fact, most aviators will tell you that they have been in love with the idea of flying since childhood. They do not know or understand why they have such an inborn desire to master the air, but frustration awaits those who ignore such a call.

Just as pilots have a love and a passion for flight, I believe most businesspeople have a love and a passion for the competitiveness and challenge of business. The "game" of business is as exciting to a businessperson as flying is to a pilot. Both may hope to succeed and prosper financially, but it is the challenge and thrill of our calling that drive us. We must take care, therefore, that we keep our businesses and successes in perspective.

Without realizing it, we may find it easy to move from totally depending on God to depending on our business for our provision and security. We often believe if we teach Sunday school, serve on church committees, or finance church projects, we are doing all we can for God and that our attitude toward our personal kingdom is healthy.

We can easily find ourselves like the rich young ruler in Luke 18, who kept all of God's commandments but could not bring himself to leave his possessions and follow Jesus. Let's be truthful here—most of us can identify with this young man. When God calls us to do something for Him, something that will cost us, we find we must override our minds, fears, and doubts to move forward with Him.

Does our kingdom or empire rule us?

Or do we have dominion over the kingdom we have built and are willing to yield it to God?

Our business talents and skills, once yielded, can help build His kingdom. As we build His house, He will build ours. When that fact motivates our work, that work becomes our ministry.

TRY GOD

Years ago, Thomas Hoving, then president and CEO of New York City's elite Tiffany Jewelers, became involved in helping drug-addicted inner-city youths come to Christ and reclaim their lives. To help fund some recovery shelters, Tiffany's designed and sold a silver lapel pin that spelled out two words: TRY GOD. The day the pins became available on Fifth Avenue, lines of eager customers stretched around the block.

TRY GOD. It is a strong, proven business principle. Just as the staid and prestigious New York jewelry establishment discovered some astonishing responses to that one simple, compelling idea and product, your business can do the same.

TRY GOD. He works. He is at work in your life, today and always.

Chapter Three

Business Lies

We met the young American couple at a restaurant in Rome. My buddy Jim and I were soldiers on leave, backpacking through the Italian countryside, seeing as much as possible on a US Army private's pay. The year was 1975, several years before I became a Christian.

The friendly young Americans were missionaries. They were there to spread the gospel of Jesus Christ, and they were curious about us and our mission in Europe. Upon learning that Jim and I intended to return to University of North Texas following our tour of duty in Germany, they asked what we planned to study. The missionaries thought Jim's major of art was "cool," yet my business major was decidedly "uncool" and was, in fact, self-serving, since I was "going after the money."

That was the first time anyone openly indicated to me that my career choice somehow might be less than worthy.

Several years after that incident, I became a Christian. By that time I also had become an all-out small businessman who thoroughly enjoyed his work, dreams, and business goals. None of this seemed to encroach on my growing love for Jesus Christ, my gratitude for all His benefits, and my growing dependence on His guidance.

We prospered: Shannon, I, and our children. My small businesses grew and flourished. We tithed our money, time, and talents. Early in our family's Christian walk, we learned that it is impossible to out-give God.

Lurking in my inner heart, however, was the growing notion the missionary girl and others like her had planted: that a passion for business and the resulting monies from a successful enterprise were somehow wrong, if not evil.

As a full-time, committed Christian, I'm not the first man or woman to wrestle with this question. Various teachers, mentors, and others we respect can mistakenly lead us to believe a series of lies about business and money. Some of these lies follow:

- Money is evil.
- It is more blessed to be poor.
- Ambition is selfish.
- Wealth produces greed, and greed produces wealth.
- Wealth is bad; we should give it all away.
- The only way to truly serve the Lord is in full-time ministry.

Is Money Bad?

As you read in chapter 1, I had all but convinced myself that my skills and enthusiasm for business must be in direct conflict with my love for and commitment to God. If business success generates financial gain and money is evil, then why was I pursuing success in business? This question undermines many businesspeople because of the underlying accusation that money, in and of itself, is evil.

The belief that money is evil is business lie number one for the Christian businessperson. Unfortunately, Christians themselves are most likely to heap condemnation on fellow Christians who are successful and prosperous in the business world.

The oft misquoted scriptures 1 Timothy 6:10, Matthew 9:16, and Luke 12:16 (love of money, rich young ruler, hoarding in silos) do not teach us that money or material possessions are bad. It is the *love* of money, the *hoarding* of possessions that will cause us problems. When the Lord asks us to give up our possessions, we should, willingly and readily. After all, everything in the earth belongs to Him, does it not? (Psalm 50:10).

God does not tell us to do something without purpose. I would encourage you to read the scriptures mentioned above, in addition to any others that might sound condemning toward success or finances. Study these scriptures to find out what God is really saying regarding money and material possessions. I believe you will find that the scriptures are there for instruction as to the *use* and *place* money is to have in our lives.

Ask yourself: What is my perception of God's will for me? Has He gifted me with business talents and skills? Has He programmed me for success? Has He enabled me to prosper, even to acquire wealth?

Then ask: Have I placed my business goals and success ahead of God in my life? Do I seek first the kingdom of God and His righteousness, as Jesus instructs us in Matthew 6:33, or do I seek first money, power, and personal ideas of success?

For the businessman or -woman who truly follows Christ, the path becomes clear. Money is not the primary *goal*, but it often is a *by-product* of dedication, success, and good stewardship. It can be used as a means to God's pathway. Money used in God's good service cannot be evil. We remain grateful to God for allowing us to be able to give to others, including those who are called to mission work.

Ask Him to help you to finance the kingdom efforts He places on your heart.

Is Ambition Bad?

I know a woman who, as a new Christian several years ago, read a book that advocated the Christian's need to "die to self." The young woman had exhibited talent in her field and gained some recognition very early. The idea of "dying to self" seemed appropriate. She knew she was hardworking, determined, and ambitious. She studied continually to perfect her professional know-how. She meant to succeed.

Once convinced she needed to "die to self," the woman convinced herself that she had to stamp out what she perceived to be her own ambitious personality. She became nearly an extremist, very averse to taking credit for ideas or even good work, melting into the background, still working hard, but believing it was more blessed to be unnoticed.

The woman became moderately successful in her career and highly successful in her quest for background status. One day, however, she received a wonderful invitation to be included in *Who's Who of American Women*. Laughing, she showed the questionnaire to her minister son before she dropped it in the trash.

"Mom," the young man began as he retrieved the material, "do you suppose God could get some glory from Christians being included in that book?"

"That was the first time in years I considered the *role* of ambition, status, and authority in a Christian's life," she told me. "By considering my personal ambitions 'bad' and by trying to stamp them out, I saw I had—at certain times—even quenched the Holy Spirit and what God was trying to do in my life."

She continued, saying, "My goal should have been that of becoming all I could become, not for my own glory (or evil ambition) but to glorify God. Actually, when your ambitions are rooted in His purposes for your life, it can only lead to His glory."

This woman has since written and edited many books, most of which have a Christian message, several of which have been on the best-seller list. Her name is Charlotte Hale Pindar, and she is my editor and advisor for this book, as well as my friend.

So we ask ourselves: How much personal ambition is too much? Only God and the individual businessperson can answer that. My observation, though, is that God often guides us via our dreams, desires, and visions. When we put God first, it's not likely that our personal ambitions can get in His way.

MORE LIES

Like Charlotte, who so often refused to stretch herself to attain new professional successes, too many other Christians also accept a variety of subtle lies. Businesspeople especially should stay alert to the many ways Satan can lead us to failure. It is his job to see that we never reach our full potential. He succeeds when we strike out. As my own walk with the Lord deepened, God began to reveal to me some of the lies that plague even godly business builders. The list of such lies and deceptions includes the following:

- Businesspeople are not spiritual.
- Businesspeople want to run the church like a corporation.
- Business success probably requires you to be crooked, selfish, or hardened.
- Businesspeople care too much about money and spend all their time chasing it.

Such lies become all too easy to accept, and I confess that at times they infected me. Often I felt guilty about my successes, and foolish and deserving of my failures. I saw myself as working hard all week for money and then worshipping God on Sunday. As the years passed, I wondered if money was my god. After all, I spent a lot of time pursuing it. We can spend years in such fruitless speculation and self-condemnation before we come to the knowledge of the truth. Too many Christians subconsciously hold fast to the negative thoughts about money and business that I held so long ago. Such thoughts have pervaded the church for centuries.

I believe these mind-sets are responsible for confusion, frustration, and low self-esteem for the follower of Christ. They result in a lack of business success and can lead us to subconsciously distance ourselves from God.

TRUTH FREES US

The knowledge that God has called us to the business world, that He has destined and equipped us for business leadership and success, provides us with a powerful mandate. No longer need we feel defensive, unsure, or unworthy of our calling. And we certainly should not be embarrassed by our success. It is time to see our destiny in the marketplace as a God-given privilege and responsibility, no less important than any other part of His divine body.

It is essential for us to understand that just as pastors and ministers must spend time with God, hear His voice, and know His will, so must we businesspeople spend time with God, hear His voice, and know His will. Just as the Holy Spirit empowers evangelists to preach and spread the gospel of Christ, so must we conduct our day-to-day business by the Spirit of God in order to achieve what God wants us to achieve in the marketplace.

We, no less than any pastor or minister, are called to take the gospel to every part of the earth. Jesus gave us that mandate, and through Him we are to accomplish it. Most of us, however, have fallen into the accepted trap of focusing primarily on our work and making Christ's mandate secondary. God wants us to devote ourselves to our partnership with Him.

The fact is that most businesspeople believe their Christian call to ministry falls far below that of a missionary or pastor. Please know that this is not the mind of Christ. He calls us to minister, whatever our station in life. We are to minister the gospel through our work. In Matthew 6:31–33 (NASB), we are reminded that this is to be our primary focus: to "seek first the kingdom of God and His righteousness."

TENT MAKERS

The apostle Paul tells us that we are to work so that we may give to others. Paul himself worked as a tent maker. He believed in the worthiness of work and even taught that those who are lazy and do not work should not eat. Paul, however, is best known as a devoted follower of Jesus Christ, one who spread Christianity to the farthest corners of the then known world.

If we, like Paul, recognize our workplace as a place to touch lives, a place where our peers can see Jesus in our lives and actions, a place from which we can give and help others, then we can see that our businesses and careers have great value to God.

We need not preach to our peers, employees, and associates. Our example and intent, our insistence on operating our business according to

God's standards, speak volumes to those around us. *Many people whose lives we touch in the workplace will never enter a church, yet through our working relationship they can see God at work in our lives.* When we focus more on what we are doing to further God's plan for the earth, we discover that our real work is to benefit His people. Business success, prosperity, and sustenance are benefits from our work but not its purpose.

Let me say that again. *Business success, prosperity, and sustenance are benefits from our work but not its purpose.*

MINISTRY

Christians must realize that God has a place and a purpose for everyone. As Christian businesspeople, we must realize our strategic place in the business world as part of our destiny within the body of Christ.

While pastors lead the church, each day businesspeople occupy the front lines of spiritual battles throughout the world. We have unique opportunities to finance ministries everywhere while shepherding our given "flock" on our jobs. We are called and created to serve Christ, just as is the pastor or evangelist. After all, only 2 percent of all Christians are on the church payroll, but God needs and expects 100 percent of us, His complete body, to fulfill the Great Commission.

Take another look at the "business lies" that affect so many Christians in the workplace. If you believe success, ambition, lofty goals, prosperity, or great dreams are somehow bad, evil, or unworthy, I challenge you to test these ideas against scripture. You will find that these thoughts are simply lies from Satan, "the accuser of the brethren."

Jesus, however, told us He came that we "may have life, and have it abundantly" (John 10:10, NASB). The apostle Paul instructed us to "Run in such a way as to get the prize" (1 Corinthians 9:24, NIV). Our prize, or success in this life, is glorious and worthy of full participation in God's kingdom on earth, and we are to use every gift and God-given ability we have in our pursuit of it.

Chapter Four

A Spiritual Purpose

What is the practical purpose of any business? It exists to solve problems. As the famous saying goes, "Find a need and fill it." There is no doubt that the innovative problem-solvers and need-fillers of this world can become unimaginably wealthy and successful.

Consider the ordinary paper clip, invented one hundred years ago by a secretary who was tired of sticking her finger whenever she used a straight pin to connect several pieces of paper. How many billions of paper clips have been used since then?

Or consider Post-it Notes, colorful little "accidental" inventions of a 3-M Corporation researcher, which for decades have decorated desks throughout the United States and the world. Our nation's history abounds in stories reflecting such innovation and ingenuity.

Then think of George Washington Carver. A black man raised by a white family as their own, choosing to cast his lot with other blacks during the bleak decades of post–Civil War reconstruction, Carver helped develop a struggling black college in the rural backwoods of Alabama. At Tuskegee Institute, a rustic school that would become world-famous through his influence, Carver studied the lowly peanut, which was easily grown and readily available. The self-directed scientist believed there must be undiscovered uses for the lowly "goober pea."

He continually prayed that God would show him new uses for the peanut. With ceaseless prayer, hard work, and persistence, his research proved that the peanut had more than three hundred industrial uses. In fact, George Washington Carver turned peanuts into mayonnaise, instant coffee, cheese, chili sauce, shampoo, bleach, axle grease, linoleum, metal polish, wood stains, adhesives, plastics, wallboard … and, yes, peanut butter.

God used George Washington Carver's genius not only in the field of science, but also in education, politics, and agriculture. Carver helped educate struggling blacks, set an important new school on its path to excellence, befriended three US presidents, consulted with Swedish royalty on agricultural methods, and counseled Mahatma Gandhi on how best to feed India's starving masses.

The man or woman who devotes his or her talents to God's uses not only may take a business to unlimited heights, but also may find his or her personal sphere of influence vastly expanded as God chooses to use our lives in ways we cannot imagine.

SPIRITUAL PURPOSE

The businessperson's ability to know God's purpose for his or her life literally transforms the individual's life as well as the business. We simply have to understand our position and place in this world, listen to God, and follow His instructions. It's that simple.

Once I understood that fully surrendering my life to God did not mean I had to leave the business world, I began asking God what He wanted me to achieve for Him. Little by little, I began to understand that we are strategically placed in business so as to fulfill our destiny as part of the body of Christ. Thus, the business's practical reason for even existing becomes transformed into something far greater than the mere sum of its parts. In other words, there is a *physical purpose* for a business on this earth, but there also is a *spiritual purpose*. The spiritual purpose is of *much* greater importance.

If you and I are called to business or a profession within the business world, we must ask ourselves, "What is God's intention for us in this field? How can He transform our daily tasks into His idea of our ultimate purpose and success?" That is for every businessman and -woman to discover. One thing is sure: our purpose will never be greater or larger than the great vision God has for us.

Spiritual Battles

Businesspeople, no less than pastors or missionaries, often find themselves on the front lines of the world's spiritual battlefields. We have unique opportunities to influence the lives of employees, clients, peers, and even our employers.

God calls us to be salt in today's corrupt and depraved world (Matthew 5:13). Salt was used in biblical times as a cleanser, disinfectant, and preservative, and, when poured into a wound, it cleanses the wound and allows it to heal. As "salt" in today's marketplace, we can pour ourselves out for others and help to cleanse away sin, vulgarity, temptation, and other evils that surround us everywhere. The marketplace today desperately needs salt.

By being close to God, we find ourselves far better equipped to make good decisions and separate the world's good from God's best. As veterans of spiritual warfare, we become confident that we can think on our feet, discern facts accurately, and speak with godly humility, truth, and authority. God trains us daily if we seek Him.

God's Anointing

As God's sons and daughters, we are anointed and equipped to overcome the problems of the world. Every hour of the day, with our Lord's ever-present help, we can combat any problem, challenge, fear, or evil we may face.

Transferring our business "ownership" to God does not mean we will never encounter the difficulties, needs, and setbacks others face. It does mean, however, that God is with us and will lead us to certain victory. Realizing that we are called to persevere in the marketplace and that He has anointed us to minister there places a very different sort of importance on one's business or career. Business exists not just to serve us or our goals, but also to glorify God in a hurting world.

God's Leading

"I have learned how to receive instructions and follow them," I recently told one of my friends who asked me what I perceived to be the *secret* of my business success.

The question arises fairly often, and my answer is always the same: "Follow God." Our churches and educational institutions often do a fine job of preparing us for life—up to a point. However, much of the world, even the Christian world, does not realize that all real success formulas taught at popular seminars feature principles that come straight from the Bible. Few men and women truly understand that we were designed and destined to achieve success.

Of course, the necessity for hard work and excellence is a given. God wants to lead us toward the training, methods, expertise, and inspiration we need. Critical components of success include knowledge, preparation, commitment, and standards of excellence. All these are critical to our achieving great exploits.

"Ask and it will be given to you," Jesus tells us. "Seek, and you will find; knock and the door will be opened to you" (Matthew 7:7, NIV). Begin asking the following questions:

- How does God see you?
- Why has He destined you for your business or career path?
- What is the spiritual purpose of your business?
- How has He uniquely equipped you?
- How should you conduct yourself?
- What specific things are you to achieve?

The more direct translation of Jesus's instructions is, "Ask and keep on asking. Seek and keep on seeking." Those who do, inevitably receive

God's leadership and divine instructions. There is no way to measure His unending faithfulness toward us.

ONE MAN'S LEADERSHIP

At first, I wondered if I was hearing God clearly. The question concerned my successful Texas flight training school, which for several years had prepared hundreds of pilots for aviation careers. It was a good business, with students coming from all parts of the United States and a high percentage of others from Europe. At our school, our students not only were trained as pilots but also were exposed to the gospel. They saw firsthand what Christianity was all about. We were proud of our students, our training, and our results.

Due to the creation of the European Union, new regulations in Europe made me wonder where our industry was headed. European laws now mandated in-country training for their licensed pilots. This cut severely into our student enrollment. For some months I asked God what we should do. Decreased enrollment did not necessarily mean our business would not survive, but it was a significant attention-grabber. Daily I asked God to reveal His intentions toward our flight school. The answer came suddenly in the form of a buyout offer from a large corporation. I recognized God's will for us, and we readily sold our business. Our agreement stated that I would remain as CEO during a one-year transition period.

We sold the aviation training business on March 31, 2001. On September 11 of that year, our nation suffered the worst aviation tragedy in our history. The attack on our country was dumbfounding. On September 12, FBI agents entered our flight school and thoroughly examined our student records. They continued to do so for the next several weeks. They found everything in order. As a Christian organization, we always had felt it important to carefully comply with immigration regulations, and we kept scrupulous records of every US and non-US student. Events of those days are burned into my memory, just as they are etched into so many other American lives. It was a time of many unforgettable events and memories.

During that time of investigation, we learned that we had refused entrance of an unqualified applicant from India to our flight school who later turned up in England with a terrorist plot to duplicate the Twin Towers tragedy on the London Tower. I was so thankful that God had prevented us from training a terrorist pilot at our flight school. He was tried in India and later hung for his crime of planning a terrorist attack.

I will never forget those vivid demonstrations of God's hand at work in my business and on my life—from the timing of the sale of the business, to the ability to produce excellent records for the FBI, to being spared from having any students who might have been a part of foreign plots.

Often we enter into the business or professional world with thoroughly practical plans, hopes, and purposes. As Christians, we're likely to ask God to bless those intentions. Once we begin steadfastly seeking God's purpose and perspective for our business, our ideas about our work begin to change.

Instead of thinking, *Should I abandon my career and train for the pulpit?* we should ask, *How can I seek God's direction for my ministry, wherever it may be?* Although some people are called to be pastors, evangelists, and missionaries, many more are called to ministry in the marketplace. We found at the aviation school that our ministry in the marketplace was to allow students from all over the world to hear, see, and experience the character of Christ while training, and to do so in a nonthreatening, noncondemning manner.

It is practical purpose combined with spiritual purpose. We do not learn these lessons in business school, nor do we usually learn them in church. But when the Holy Spirit becomes our teacher and the Bible becomes our textbook, we have everything we will ever need.

Section Two

Success

Let the Lord be magnified, who takes
pleasure in the prosperity of His servant.
—Psalm 35:27 (AMP)

Chapter Five

Called to Increase

"If you're dealing with a spirit of poverty, please stand up." In a church service several years ago, the pastor was speaking to a number of us—including me. As several strugglers slowly rose to their feet, I stood up too. Some people around me looked surprised. Though I was well dressed and considered successful by most, God and I knew all too well how strongly I had been motivated in business by a fear of poverty.

Most who stood that day were dealing with daily bill-paying issues, the day-to-day financial struggles that keep many in financial bondage. I stood because I found that I was driven to success by a fear of financial struggle. I had been there before and did not want to revisit it. I stood up that day thinking, *I want to deal with this fear of poverty if that's what's driving me.*

Like so many others, I had by now sincerely committed my life and my business to God. In my earlier walk as a Christian, I always had asked the Lord to bless my business plans or decisions. But the Texas-style Damascus Road experience I had on that rainy afternoon a few years earlier had changed all that. At that point, having come to the end of myself and my previous, earlier successes, I finally turned everything about my business over to God. Instead of asking Him to "bless my steps," I asked Him to show me "where to step." This new approach to my life created some amazing and life-stretching results for me and my family.

A steep learning curve followed. I came to realize that God has programmed us to succeed, but not apart from Him. He wants to increase the gifts and talents He placed in us before our birth. He brought Abraham Lincoln out of a log cabin in the wilderness to a place of high purpose in a time of American crisis. He transformed another Abraham, the Abraham of the Bible, into an extremely wealthy rancher, and far beyond that—appointing him to become "a father of nations." So closely did Abraham walk with Jehovah that the Bible calls him "a friend of God."

In Deuteronomy 8:18 (AMP), we learn "it is He [God] who gives you the power to get wealth." Did God bestow that power on Abraham? Does divine intimacy lead to prosperity and personal power in our world today? And if becoming wealthy/successful/powerful in that way is okay, have we the right and even the obligation to pursue it? If so, why? For what purpose?

I believe the Holy Spirit not only woos us to our salvation, but thereafter also woos us into closer relationships with our Father God. The career or business we create, nurture, and labor over either becomes a barrier to our closest possible relationship to God, or it can lead us ever closer to Him as we seek Him in every aspect of our life.

The business or career committed to His kingdom, just as the life that is turned over to its Creator, is destined for success in every sense of the word. The late Dr. E. Stanley Jones, noted Methodist evangelist, preacher, and author, reminded us that when God creates an acorn, He intends it to grow into a mighty oak tree. Thus the acorn-sized talents of an ordinary man or woman, placed in God's hands, can flower and spread in amazing and unimaginable ways. As the Bible tells us, God can choose any among us to stand before kings.

Read the Bible, and again and again and you will see that "with God all things are possible" (Matthew 19:26, NASB). This is a true statement and a promise for each of us. Even a lack of education, prestige, money, friends, possessions, or good health does not prevent the God-in-us from succeeding. He has built Himself into us, stamped us with His divine DNA, made us in His very image.

FAILURE AND SUCCESS

Jesus warned us that "apart from Me you can do nothing" (John 15:5, NIV). To become all He intends us to be, we must, like Abraham, draw closer and closer to God. To become a true Christian businessman or businesswoman, rather than a Christian who simply has built a business or career, is to turn that endeavor over to the lover of our soul (our Lord) as we attempt to follow Him in all our ways. Some call God their partner. I'd rather call myself His partner, one called according to His purposes.

Numerous businesspeople that many of us know and recognize have turned their businesses over to God finally and completely, often achieving spectacular successes. They become people Jesus likened to a city set upon a hill, whose light cannot be hidden (Matthew 5:14). Two such businessmen that come to mind, the late R. G. LeTourneau and Conrad Hilton, each continuously led by God, became world changers and legends standing tall above most other Christians of their era.

R. G. LeTourneau—Earth Mover

LeTourneau, the famed inventor and manufacturer of earth-moving machines, offshore oil drilling rigs, and other cutting-edge industrial devices, became a problem-solving genius, leaping ahead of others in his constant ability to invent major labor-saving, time-saving, and money-saving machines, literally capable of moving mountains or diverting rivers. The man lacked even a high school education and confessed that he had no preparation or skill for business. Undeniably he was a mechanical and engineering genius and an incredibly gifted inventor. Early in his career, LeTourneau understood that he had to turn over to God every segment of his life. His business became God's business.

LeTourneau made mistakes, sometimes very costly mistakes, as he expanded his personal vision and improved his skills. But he never made

41

the most common mistake of all: underestimating himself to the point that he doubted God's ability to work through him.

LeTourneau learned to leave every business problem, decision, and instruction to God. Machines he designed and manufactured literally "made the high places low and the rough places plain." He created California roads by cutting through rock outcrops, and he built platforms on stilts planted in ocean waters from which oil could be harvested. Uses for his heavy tools are too many to relate—they changed the face of our globe.

Despite his growing record of successes, Robert G. LeTourneau never felt tempted to cut the divine umbilical cord that tied him to the nourishment and security of his heavenly Father. Indeed, he feared severing that cord. "I'll admit that at one time," he said, "I feared my love of machines was becoming an obsession that was taking me away from my love of God. I went to Him for help and was reassured. I was just a mechanic striving to translate His laws in terms of machinery, and as long as I understood I was just His follower, and didn't get to thinking I was operating under my own head of steam, I was on the right track."[ii]

During World War II, LeTourneau saw his huge machinery help turn the tide of battle as rigs capable of doing the work of one hundred men swiftly and efficiently created new roads, airstrips, or passages; moved tons of war wreckage; filled swamplands; and ultimately facilitated the advancement of Allied forces to victory. With thousands of his machines in Europe, Africa, and Asia, LeTourneau made a staggeringly huge contribution to the war's outcome. As with all his successes, he gave God the credit.

His contributions at a crucial point in world history actually began years earlier, the night after LeTourneau's first child, a baby son, died in the terrible 1917 influenza epidemic. The heartbroken father questioned God as to why committed Christians should be so punished. "We have worked so hard," cried the anguished young father. "Oh, where have we gone wrong?" Soon, he heard God's answer: "My child, you have been working hard for material things when you should have been working for spiritual things."[iii] Rather than punishing LeTourneau, God used the loss of his son to draw the young father's heart to Himself, and in this case, to open LeTourneau's eyes to his selfish actions. Reviewing his life, LeTourneau saw he had been a token Christian, really serving himself and his own conscience, rather than serving God. He testified later that he came to see that God loves us so much that He wants us to love Him in return. "He wants us to cooperate with His program."[iv]

LeTourneau adopted a scripture: "Seek ye first the kingdom of God and His righteousness; and all these things shall be added unto you" (Matthew 6:33, KJV). Measured against that commandment, the man could see he had been seeking his own way of life. From that day forward, he continued to measure his life and work against that scripture, preaching it whenever he addressed a group.

My own turning point, that unforgettable day in the rain, echoed that of LeTourneau's and so many other Christians of every other generation. Jesus preached about Himself that unless a kernel of wheat falls into the ground and dies, it cannot bear much fruit (John 12:24). Until we allow our pride, ownership, and personal ambition to fall into the ground and die, we cannot bear much fruit or see significant increase in our life and our work.

God wants us to increase, and we will, beyond anything we can imagine, when we partner with Him. The apostle John wrote, "Beloved, I pray that you may prosper and be in good health, just as your soul prospers" (3 John 1:2, NKJV). If we desire that God have His way in our lives, we desire to come into that unity of purpose that fulfills God's plans for our prosperity. The great God who gave humanity dominion over all the earth has not called us to a small life and limited effectiveness. Once yoked with Jesus Christ, we begin to learn that truly all things are possible. Putting our ownership aside, and yielding to the One who knew us in our mother's womb, we learn how to become molded into His vision for us—a vision far greater than we can imagine for ourselves.

OVERCOMING PROBLEMS

Even in the yielded life, ordinary earthly problems will certainly still arise. These can range from daily irritations to severe tragedies, such as financial ruin or the loss of a loved one. The practical thing to do about these problems, as LeTourneau noted, is to take them to God in prayer and then walk away from them: "The Lord can't help you if you insist on carrying your problems with you. Leave them with Him and they are no longer yours, but His."[v]

I found leaving hard business problems in God's lap and walking away to be more difficult than it sounds. It is said that we often give our problems to God in prayer at 6:30 a.m., but we have taken them back by 8:30 a.m. if we are not careful. The results of giving our cares and problems to God, however, prove practical indeed. A calm, peaceful, rested mind, after all, is the most fertile field in which new ideas and solutions can sprout. But to trust God to solve hard problems sometimes seems, to many of us, like copping out. After all, if it's our business or career, why should we expect Him to take over when we are facing immense problems?

Only the confidence we have in Him, the knowledge that He is able, that His love for us is beyond all we can imagine, and that His mercies are new every morning, can answer that. To trust Him with "my" ideas, "my" business standing, "my" ultimate success soon teaches me the fundamental truth that everything we are and all we have comes from our Father.

PARTNERSHIP WITH GOD

Why then do so few Christian businesspeople ever go into the divine partnership that LeTourneau and others like him knew? Why do so many of us continue to struggle, even fail, or live so far beneath our privileges?

Often it is because we feel unworthy. We cannot envision the potential for a God-given high calling or megasuccess in business. Unless we know and relate to our heavenly Father and His Son, there can be no possibility of accomplishing the highest purposes for which He created us.

Sure, you can point to talented and successful individuals who boast they "did it my way." God's increase, however, includes far more than noteworthy business or career accomplishments or monetary enrichment.

God's intention for increasing and prospering each one of His children who seek first His kingdom and His righteousness is for wealth, health, healing, wholeness, and success on a scope we cannot imagine. Our God-produced wealth, as LeTourneau saw, can help solve worldwide problems; contribute to winning a world war; supply missionaries; found a Bible School and a technical college; supply jobs and futures for thousands of men, women, and struggling communities; help end poverty for individuals around the globe; and leave the greatest legacy of all. LeTourneau set the example for his four sons and one daughter and their families, all of whom have dedicated their lives to Christian service. And he set an example for all of us too.

There is no doubt that God increased R. G. LeTourneau and gave him power to gain wealth. At one point, his wife, Evelyn, protested when her husband decided they should give half of their income to God—because that would leave them with *too much money* for one household. They began increasing their giving, and by the end of his career, LeTourneau and his family were giving God 90 percent of their income and living on the remaining 10 percent.

The question arises: Can any business—even my business—prosper to the amazing extent that LeTourneau's did? To the level that we place our trust in God, we can be sure that He can and will trust us with wealth and increase. From earth's beginning, that has been His plan.

Although many of us may hold degrees from excellent schools, such wisdom is not learned at a university. Good schools may give us knowledge, but it is God who will give us wisdom. In His word, the Bible, He reveals to us time-enduring principles for success in life. Such training can build LeTourneau-sized success. God's principles for success remain eternally simple, as R. G. LeTourneau's and Conrad Hilton's lives and business careers vividly illustrate.

CHAPTER SIX

THE SIMPLICITY OF ACHIEVEMENT AND SUCCESS

Yes, I said *simple*—but not necessarily *easy*. Today's business- and career-oriented individuals, believers and nonbelievers alike, have access to and knowledge of seemingly every possible road map to success. Seminars, trainers, coaches, Internet courses, business retreats, and strategy sessions number among the dozens of ways to catch the golden ring. Hard work, consistency, determination, worthy mentoring, and effective investment strategies and cash-raising techniques … the list seems endless in our business-driven, technology-fueled information age.

Actually, the pathway to achieving personal and business success always has been plain and simple. It is as simple as one's decision to obey God. Obedience to Him, simplistic and quaint as that may sound, time and again has proved to be a powerful juggernaut, an immense liftoff to the stars. Quite simply, it really is God who gives us the power to obtain every sort of wealth (Deuteronomy 8:18).

Why, then, do so many Christians choose to live lives of mediocrity? Why the small thinking? Why the piddling results and endless excuses from even born-again, spirit-filled sons and daughters of our Almighty God? Why the fear, anxiety, and low self-worth among those who know they were bought for an unthinkable price and that God has created us in His image and set us only a little lower than His angels?

That's a lot to get ahold of, and too few ever do. The way to the great things of God and to God Himself is the road of obedience. The man or woman who obeys God's instructions and adopts His principles has no need to strive for success and personal gain. Jesus taught us that all the Father has is ours (Luke 15:31).

HILTON HOTELS

The late Conrad Hilton, hotel magnate, a man who obviously knew plenty about business, high achievement, far-reaching vision, money, and finance, recognized that he did not learn his dizzying success practices in business school.

Unlike Hilton, I studied business in college and only later learned to rely on the same best-selling business textbook Conrad Hilton had used throughout his entire business career—the Bible. That book of all books contains not only every proven success principle devised by the One who created us, but also some seven thousand promises from God to us. The book of Proverbs alone is full of all the success information a business, career, or life could possibly need. Each of the hundreds of business/success/motivational bestsellers that roll off the presses each year promotes well-proven principles and practices first laid out for us in the Bible.

Conrad Hilton, the oldest son of Christian parents, was trained early to follow Christ and His teachings. As Hilton was growing up in the late 1800s in the rough territory that later became New Mexico, his pioneer mother, a devout woman, taught her children to turn to God for every answer and to call on Him for every need. She instructed her son to pray daily. That habit, instilled early, led Conrad Hilton to consult God daily about everything, large or small, throughout his life. Whether he was at home or out of town, he always found a church nearby and began his day by going to that church and praying.

Frontier life, almost unimaginably hard and boring from today's perspective, would seem to foster a total dependence on God. Long hours of hard physical labor, scarcity of comforts, uncertain access to provisions and sometimes even needs such as proper schooling would either make one exceedingly self-reliant or teach one to rely on God. Fortunately for Hilton, his family chose the latter course.

The story of Conrad Hilton's life, a Horatio Alger–type success story, makes for riveting reading. From frontier-style beginnings, he went on to found, own, and manage some of the world's most comfortable, service-oriented, and profitable hotels in history. He led an apparently charmed life, rising in influence and success decade by decade throughout his life. He worked as hard as a sledgehammer, leaped toward new challenges and opportunities, yet despite his apparent daring actions, he almost never lost in the high-risk career path he chose to follow.

The secret of his success? Conrad Hilton always looked to God. His mother saw to that. Once, the story goes, she saw him sketching a tall building with "Hilton" spread across its façade, and she asked, "Something new?"

"I'm putting a dream on paper," he replied. "Maybe it's time to go all out. This time I'm really going big. And the first thing I need to do is raise a million dollars." As always, Hilton's mother had a more practical suggestion: "If you are serious, son, the first thing you'd better do is pray about it."[vi] The hotelier's mother always had one answer for everything—prayer.

The apostle Paul told his followers to put on the mind of Christ. That mind purposed to do the will of the Father. Those who pray about everything learn how to ask, how to expect, how to receive, and above all, how to listen to Him. Both R. G. LeTourneau and Conrad Hilton told of hearing God speak to their inner spirits. They spoke of specific answers to specific problems or needs suddenly crowding into their minds. Those methods, simple as our normal questions, answers, and conversations, worked for these men and countless others.

These days too few of us find time for human–God conversation. We are addicted to activity: cell phones, iPods, iPads, e-mail, Facebook, and the like. We are truly in a high-speed race in this life, communicating with everyone but God.

Even a century ago, after the industrial revolution, the poet Wordsworth observed a change in society. He expressed it as "getting and spending we lay waste our powers." Spending time with God in prayer helps us learn to live without fear and anxiety, and it allows us to avoid many detours and failures we would otherwise experience. Read Philippians 4:6. God does not lead us into failure. He gives us the freedom to choose it. I have found that prayer habits sustained throughout life teach us to discipline ourselves to necessary work, and we can then expect to overcome tough times, hard labor, and even tragedies and loss. Prayer, that simple but secure link between man and God, proves the most powerful and never-failing protection a man or woman can adopt.

DREAM BIG

Late in his life, Conrad Hilton's son Barron asked his father the secret to his many successes. Hilton's response was to *work hard* and *pray*. Barron, however, insisted there must be something more. He knew plenty of people who prayed and worked hard, yet never attained much in life. After thinking about it further, Hilton added another part to the secret. He told his son to *dream big*.

He knew, of course, the Author of his big dreams and plans. He knew who provided his faith, vision, and courage to pursue his dreams. Think big. Act big. Dream big. Be honest. Those were the added tenets, pathways that led out from Hilton's lifelong prayer habits.

Big dreams can be derived from faithful prayer. As Hilton explained, those big dreams must line up with "progress, human and divine, or you are wasting your prayers. It has to be backed with work and faith, or it has no hands and feet."[vii]

Many years earlier, he had dreamed of someday owning the famed Waldorf Astoria Hotel, the New York City landmark he dubbed "the greatest of them all." He described some of what it took to acquire, after many years of dreaming and steady preparation, the crown jewel of his hotel chain.

During the final crucial days before "the greatest" became a Hilton hotel, Conrad Hilton attended church at six thirty each morning. "It had taken a lot of prayer," he related. "No matter how late we worked at night, I started the day on my knees."[viii]

Mr. Hilton believed Jesus's instructions to us: "Therefore I tell you, whatever you ask for in prayer, believe that you have received it, and it will be yours" (Mark 11:24, NIV).

A MIND-SET FOR SUCCESS

Ask yourself: What makes the difference between successful businesspeople and those who struggle? Why will a small business survive for several years and then suddenly gain resounding success? Why can some businesspeople take almost any struggling business, large or small, and turn it around?

And: Why are some businesspeople paid very large sums of money? Do they work harder than others, or is their ability to make the profitable decisions for their company recognized and greatly valued?

Business skills in management, finance, negotiation, etc., are teachable and obtainable skills for most people. However, even when these are coupled with hard work and determination, only moderate success is normally achieved. As N. R. Stevenson, my entrepreneurial father, once told me when I was a young man, "There are always plenty of smart people that work hard."

Christians, however, have an advantage over the rest of the world, yet they often fail to recognize or use it. This advantage can take a company from mediocrity to success, a career from "going nowhere fast" to one filled with excitement and achievement.

When you realize the simplicity of achieving success, you will be amazed at the ease of it all. It is true and correct that a million-dollar deal is not really any more difficult to achieve than a thousand-dollar deal. It depends on you and where your sights are set. Even more amazing is the fact that more people do not achieve personal success, because most people are not mentally or spiritually open to success, or they are not willing to do what is necessary to succeed.

The components of success include knowledge, preparation, commitment, and excellence. These are things we should be taught at home, in school, or on the job. They are critically important to our success. However, in order to really achieve fulfillment and success in our work, we need to understand

- who we are in the eyes of God,
- why we like the competitiveness and combativeness of business,
- why He created us this way,
- how He expects us to conduct ourselves,
- what He expects us to achieve, and
- how we are to achieve it all.

Most of what I have learned about doing business by following God has been through digging into the Bible, speaking with successful Christian businesspeople, experiencing success and failure, and seeking God through prayer. While these chapters may mentor you somewhat, it is my hope and expectation that you will come to know and communicate with the mentor given to us by God—His Holy Spirit.

CHAPTER SEVEN

EARTHLY SUSTENANCE OR KINGDOM OF WEALTH?

He came from a north Georgia hamlet and had little schooling, but he really loved the Lord. He baked bread for a livelihood. He found his work stifling, because he had a restless spirit and dreamed of going out, anywhere, to somehow serve the Lord.

"I prayed, 'Give us this day our daily bread,'" Lewis said. "Jesus taught us to pray for bread. I had to sell bread to support my family. It was the only work I knew."

This baker, so unhappy in his work, began to pray for God to deliver him from the monotony of his small-town life, where he baked the same loaves of bread six days a week. He felt stuck. He saw no way out.

In time, Lewis began to pray for the "impossible." If God would allow him to retire at age fifty, he would devote the rest of his life to lay ministry. This was a large prayer for a small bakery owner in a small town to pray. But this notion of the "impossible" Lewis was asking God to provide increased his faith.

Soon Lewis found himself reaching out to his customers, who were old friends, with words of encouragement. At times he even offered a quick prayer or reminded them of a scripture verse that spoke to their need.

Lewis could not have told you that he had entered into marketplace ministry; he had never heard of that term. He simply placed a Bible near the booths where people had their coffee and sweet roll and kept tracts beside the napkin dispensers, and from time to time these seeds would sprout. When customers paused to talk, Lewis always made time to listen.

He continued to pray the "impossible" prayer. "Lord, if you let me retire at fifty, I promise I'll go where you want me to go, do what you ask me to do, and say what you tell me to say." Still, nothing changed—nothing, that is, except Lewis.

Somebody suggested starting a Bible study before work if Lewis would open up the bakery. Soon the booths were filling up, early on Tuesday mornings while the first loaves of bread were cooling. Lewis stayed busy running back and forth to the ovens, but he listened to the other fellows and kept the coffee and hot rolls coming.

One day Lewis realized that his small bakery had become a small mission field. His employees listened in on the Bible talk. Several of those in the booths got saved. Because a business with good foot traffic attracts even more business, the bakery prospered. One day Lewis's group dedicated his bakery to the Lord. They asked God to bless each person who came through its doors and to bless Lewis for offering his customers the real bread ... the Bread of Life.

MORE THAN MERE SUSTENANCE

This is a great story of how one ordinary man stopped working for mere sustenance, his only means of supporting his family, and instead entered into kingdom work in a hole-in-the-wall bakery in a one-stoplight town.

There's much more to the story, of course. Lewis had become happy with all he could see God doing in his work and on his premises. No longer did he chafe at his perceived confinement and restraints. He all but forgot about his "impossible" prayer.

Then the dime store next door closed its doors, and Lewis decided to expand into the larger space. His sons came in to learn the business, and they began to offer meals. Meanwhile, Alma, Lewis's thrifty wife, put a down payment on some derelict apartment buildings with a little household money she had set aside. Lewis grumbled because they not only had to deal with his fast-growing bakery and café but were also hustling to clean, paint, and repair those old buildings. It took more than a year of their spare time. Lewis said, "It liked to have killed the whole family."

When they sold those apartments, however, the profits made Lewis and Alma grateful to God. What a windfall! But Lewis didn't like it when his wife wanted to take part of that money for a down payment on some good-for-nothing rocky, barren acreage she had located. They argued, then prayed, and then went ahead and bought it. (Lewis hoped she wasn't getting too interested in real estate!)

When developers came to build the town's first strip mall, guess whose acreage they bought? That event came out of the blue, something nobody had dreamed of. Lewis's fiftieth birthday arrived several months later. By then his boys were running the bakery and café. Thanks to God and to his wife's shrewd investing, Lewis and Alma could retire and live off their investments.

Lewis, still a small-town fellow with limited formal education, became a well-known Christian speaker. His message to other businessmen and -women focused on trusting God instead of using all their efforts in pursuing personal wealth and success.

"Jesus taught us to pray each day for that day's bread," Lewis often said. "Bread to give us strength. Bread to nourish us. But most of us don't want plain old bread. We want lemon pie or chocolate cake. We spend all our time and money going after what we want, not what God wants."

Lewis and Alma had discovered the Christian's greatest secret. Working for mere sustenance often becomes laborious, stressful, and confining, while working to build God's kingdom, even when the work is equally labor-intensive, always builds an individual's character, widens his spiritual and mental horizons, and feeds his life and heart with all good things.

As Christians, we need to think right ... we need to think with a Godlike mind-set. Financial gain is not the *goal* but rather a *by-product* of a prosperous and successful business. God made us like Himself to be builders, creators, and restorers. He did not create us just to toil away at a job. According to the Bible, He created us to rule the earth, to be in relationship with it, and to expand His spiritual kingdom on it.

Just as God gave Adam dominion over the Garden of Eden and all the contents of this earth, He gives us dominion and oversight over all He has placed under our stewardship. Homes, businesses, financial holdings, lands, and property are ours not in perpetuity, but placed by God into our receivership for kingdom purposes. Ideally, today's work should not just produce *personal enrichment* but also create *eternal glory*.

So what purpose drives *your* work, career, or profession? Let us compare the world's attitudes to those God set forth in the Holy Bible:

> *The World says:* we must work for food and shelter.
> *The Bible says:* our work has a higher purpose.
> *The World says:* hard work produces success and prosperity.
> *The Bible says:* God gives us power to get wealth.
> *The World says:* God helps those who help themselves.
> *The Bible says:* we are to build God's kingdom through our work.

In short, we are not to accept the world's thinking, but are called to seek the wisdom, direction, and purposes of God. As we go about God's business, we will discover sustenance issues taking care of themselves.

CARS FOR GOD

A used-car lot owner in Tennessee fully understood those principles. A small-business owner at first, he worked hard and traveled far to find vehicles he could clean, repair, and make roadworthy. He was a good mechanic who knew virtually every make of automobile, but a lot of sweat and effort went into rebuilding vehicles that, in the end, did not yield much monetary gain.

Fred bought his first car for two hundred dollars. "Took more than that to fix it up for sale," he said, laughing. But he dedicated his lot to the Lord, consulted God about every junker he bought, and prayed for each car once it was ready for sale.

Not too many years after that initial investment, Fred was making a good living. He tithed and gave to God's work, but he felt there was still more for him to do. One day he prayed that God would send ministers to his used-car lot, and that he would be able to give them reliable vehicles for their use. "The next day, God took me up on the prayer," he related. "Guess He didn't want me to forget or back out on my promise." He laughed.

Fred led the pastor, a man he did not know, to several vehicles he felt sure would be suitable. "If money didn't matter, which one would you choose?" he asked.

"That one," the man replied, pointing to the best car on the lot.

"It was my showpiece," Fred related. "The best, most expensive car we had, polished and shined to perfection. I knew the man didn't intend to buy that car, knew he didn't have the money, and for a moment I wavered. I wasn't yet financially ready to give a car away, I told God, and anyhow, this fellow had no idea about my plan. But he was a pastor, even if he wasn't in our denomination, so I told him he could have the car for free."

Fred recalled the man's amazement and joy, his thrilled acceptance of an unearned vehicle. "Myself? I felt a little sick," Fred said. "I walked back to my office after the fellow drove away, mentally thinking how many other clunkers I'd have to fix up to make up for this one car. Then God jolted me with a reminder of something I had not earned either—my salvation."

That first giveaway transaction did not produce immediate joy in his heart, Fred admits. "I told the Lord, please don't send so many that it puts me out of business," he recalled. Actually, as Fred dedicated not only his automobiles but all his business dealings to God, he found he had eased into full-time kingdom work. Decades later, he has given away countless used and new cars to be used in God's work. Each vehicle and its owner are prayed for and anointed for service.

Today, Fred owns two major dealerships, a bank, and a mortgage company. He became a church and civic leader, but the positions he prizes are those advising and directing several major ministries and two Christian colleges. Here is a fine example of how a God-directed two-hundred-dollar investment can multiply and succeed for His kingdom—and how a man who takes dominion over even the smallest, least-important business in town can, with God's help, significantly increase His kingdom.

A HOUSE DIVIDED

Abraham Lincoln, America's president during the anguishing Civil War years, said, "A house divided against itself cannot stand." Most recall that famous statement, but few realize Lincoln was quoting the words of Jesus Christ (Mark 3:25).

Christian business owners, entrepreneurs, or professionals who have dedicated their lives to God and are serious about following Christ inevitably come, if they are like I was, to a place where nothing in their business seems to work anymore. There I was, confused, angry, humiliated, despairing, and weeping in the rain, not knowing that my "house," my inner man, was sharply divided against itself and could no longer stand.

I see that moment in the rain and mud as one of the most God-blessed experiences of my life. It began the re-formation of a man who, like Lewis and Fred and so many others, has prayed that his life hold greater meaning.

Why God chooses to expand His kingdom through men and women like you and me is hard to understand. We know, however, that God always has used those who are faithful, those who obey, and those who listen for His voice. He can use the simplest and humblest among us to accomplish great exploits. By carrying the gospel to every nation on earth, we are working alongside the Lord to expand His kingdom. He has called us, as Christians and as businesspeople, to build, establish, and carry out His purposes.

Our role as businessmen and -women holds high importance. He has trusted us with much. But we must realize that we cannot build two kingdoms. Either we choose to labor for our personal kingdom of sustenance and self-preservation, or we work here and now for the eternal kingdom of God. We businesspeople must choose this day which kingdom we will build. Truly, a house or life divided against itself cannot stand.

CHAPTER EIGHT

GIVING BACK: STEWARDSHIP AND SUCCESS

Any business or profession, once turned over to God, becomes the most exciting adventure one could undertake. For most of us, maybe all of us, a steep learning curve is involved. Utilizing biblical instructions and principles, we begin to learn business from God's perspective.

As Christian businesspeople we love the Lord, and we desire to do His will, but this commitment continually tests us. God will cause us to reach higher, work harder, and pray more to achieve whatever He has set before us to achieve (i.e., to succeed).

Most of the world desires success in terms of money, power, fame, and material wealth. Such success can be trivial, empty, and transitory. This kind of success often mocks its owner with feelings of dissatisfaction, restlessness, and depression. Godly success, however costly it may seem, richly rewards us in countless tangible and intangible ways. God-given success is real, true, and fulfilling.

BUSINESS MANAGEMENT 101

Toss aside the dozens of business management books we all buy and read, and get your instructions from the Bible. As was stated earlier, every success principle other books teach can be found in God's word. What business school professors call "management," God calls "stewardship," and He has chosen us to be His stewards. A steward is defined as "one entrusted with the management of the affairs of others."[ix] Throughout the Bible, we are instructed to act as good stewards of all that has been entrusted to us.

From Adam's experiences in the Garden of Eden to the instructions of Jesus before He departed, God repeatedly tells us that He has placed the earth and all it contains into our hands for His purposes. He expects us to act, on His behalf, as His ambassadors and stewards.

Obviously, we must recognize that anything we build on His earth is for God, not ourselves. Thus our business and all our talents, great or small, ordinary or brilliant, belong to Him and serve as a conduit for His intentions.

Taking it still further, you can even say that when you walk into your office, you are in your place of ministry. When we answer our phone, text or e-mail our peers, interact with others, and manage money, we act as God's ambassadors and stewards. Overseeing, managing, and serving are a part of fulfilling His purposes in our business lives.

GIVING BACK

Distribution of the resources of both time and money that God places in our hands is a responsibility and a form of stewardship. Biblical stewardship of money is a broad subject demanding much more than a chapter in this or any other book. It is a serious subject and is important to God. In fact, the Bible contains more verses relating to money than any other subject. The resource of time is often overlooked, but serious consideration should be given to our own views of time as a stewardship issue. Do we *give financially* is one question to ask ourselves. But we also should ask ourselves if we *give our time* to others in mentoring, teaching, or helping those in need.

Many of the current and historical business success stories in America sprang from people who adamantly believed that the principle of *giving back* is a key to success in the business world. I am not necessarily speaking of just Christians, but across-the-board sharp, gifted, hardworking men and women who have observed the importance of the principle of giving firsthand.

One great historical entrepreneur, Andrew Carnegie, even wrote a book on the subject titled *The Gospel of Wealth*, wherein he discusses the responsibility of those who are fortunate enough to obtain wealth. Possibly the wealthiest man in the world during his era, he not only wrote on the subject, but he also lived it—giving the vast majority of his fortune to charitable organizations. It was his money that was used to bring the public library to many communities in the United States and other countries. Contrary to rumor, he did leave an estate to his family as well, and they have continued to exercise his charitable practices and principles.

As Christians, we should know that not only is giving a good principle and practice for all to follow … it also is biblical. As with all other successful business principles taught in the world, the important principle of giving also originates in the Bible. Some of the many scriptures that instruct us to give include Acts 20:35, Proverbs 11:24–25, Luke 12:34, 1 Timothy 6:18–19, Malachi 3:8–10, and Matthew 25:35–45.

"GOERS" AND "SENDERS"

Reading and understanding these scriptures are vital to the Christian businessperson. As followers of Christ, we can easily understand His giving up a carpentry business to go into ministry. We can even relate to it. We all have friends who have done the same, giving up lucrative careers to go into ministry at God's calling. However, Jesus also gave up His life as a sacrifice for our salvation. I never have died for anyone, nor has the Lord asked me to do so. Yet He has made it clear in His word that we are to act on His behalf, as His representatives on this earth. That means providing for the underprivileged and fulfilling the Great Commission Jesus described in Matthew 28:19. This may mean giving up time and money for His purposes.

A business friend of mine, John Hitt, who at one time owned a small airline company and loved missionary work, once told me: "Regarding missions, you have the 'goers' and the 'senders.'" As businesspeople, we have a responsibility to be the senders.

MONEY AND OUR HEART

Money issues expose a person's heart. It often is said that one can look in a person's checkbook and quickly find out where his or her heart is. There is truth to that statement. Are we spending our monies on ourselves and our pleasures without regard to God's purposes for money under our stewardship?

There is a story in the Bible of a young man who actually met Jesus face-to-face. He was invited to follow Him, perhaps to become one of the disciples. This young man had lived a righteous life. He also had many possessions. All that was required for the young man to join with Jesus was that he give up his wealth. The young man felt greatly grieved because he could not let go of his wealth, become economically vulnerable, and walk hand-in-hand with Jesus.

We all deal with this issue. The choice of "material security" versus "spiritual purpose" is a very hard issue. It is a matter of trust … trust in God. If He wants us to give up something that is important to us, can we believe that it is for a greater purpose? Can we truly trust Him to provide us with what we need as we give freely when He calls us to? The "wealth" of the rich young ruler was not the problem. The fact that he was unwilling to place his wealth under the jurisdiction of Christ was the issue. Did he refuse due to fear? Or was it due to a love of feeling secure and living comfortably?

If we are able to grasp that God owns and provides everything on the earth, and that we are simply His stewards, giving becomes much easier for us. We learn to trust God with everything.

DEVELOPING STEWARDSHIP

The process of becoming a worthy steward of one's business and all else God entrusts to us remains a constant throughout our life. Our hearts and habits change. We measure our natures and behaviors against God's word. We begin to develop new life rules, as God directs, to apply to our particular situations.

These four attitudinal changes help bring God's will into our lives and choices:

1. Recognize that everything belongs to God. We are His stewards. He will equip us for management of the resources He puts into our hands.
2. Inventory the gifts, talents, and resources God has given us. Know our sphere of stewardship. Be willing for God to expand our capabilities as He desires.
3. Begin using the gifts, talents, and financial resources God has entrusted to us. "Faith, if it has no works, is dead" (James 2:17, NAS).
4. Study the principles of stewardship, and fortify our life by putting them into action.

As "stewards" for Christ, we are to exercise wisdom and judgment. Being "willing to give" does not mean that we "give simply to give." We are to ask in prayer and study for God to reveal the specific uses He has for the financial resources He has placed into our hands.

MILLIONAIRES

There is a television show in the United States and United Kingdom titled *Who Wants to Be a Millionaire?* When I was giving a talk on kingdom finances to a small church group, I began by asking that question: "Who wants to be a millionaire?" Believe me, this got their attention. Only a few raised their hands, but I could read the minds of the others as they questioned their judgment in asking such a materialistic-minded person to teach in their midst. After all, this was a "spiritual" group.

By the end of the course and after understanding the concept of stewardship verses ownership, several in the audience came to me and said they now wanted to join the group that said they wanted to be millionaires. They had realized that having financial resources actually could increase their ability to promote the gospel and bless the families of the earth by being good stewards for God.

You see, I personally believe God is looking for stewards … men and women He can trust to do what He wants with His finances. When we give according to His will, we often find that our income, and therefore our stewardship, increases. We should all strive to find ourselves worthy to become "chief stewards," shouldn't we?

GIVING ATTITUDES

While becoming financially prosperous so as to have the ability to give "big" into God's work on this earth is a worthwhile goal, we must realize that giving is an attitude of the heart. The Lord knows your heart. He alone knows if you have an "ownership" problem with finances. The amount of your giving does not impress God so much as the *attitude* behind your giving. This idea is displayed in the story of the widow's mite (Luke 21:2), when Jesus states that the widow's small, private gift is more worthy than the larger financial gifts given by those in public view.

How many times have we harbored the thought that if we were wealthy we would become better givers? We must realize that what we do with our finances today is a reflection of our attitude toward money, God, and stewardship. It also indicates what our attitude will be when we do begin to prosper financially. If we cannot give out of our means today, we likely have an issue of ownership and trust in our relationship with God, and that issue will continue to be the same until we purposefully change it.

I believe that the New Testament scriptures show us that God is not happy with the Old Testament 90/10 split. The 10 percent tithe was the amount required by the Law. As New Testament Christians, we must realize that we cannot simply give 10 percent to the church and then think we are "off the hook" in our giving. No, the Lord makes it clear that it is all His. Sometimes, we are to give much more than 10 percent (Acts 4:34).

We should be careful not to make or create a "rule" in this area. One person may feel directed by the Lord to give all he has to a ministry, but this does not automatically mean that you and all other Christians must do the same. Each situation is different. He may require you to give 10 percent at times, and 50 percent at other times. You may become like R. G. LeTourneau and give 90 percent of your income and live on 10 percent. How exciting would that be?

In summation, we must be willing stewards of His finances. After all, it is His money, isn't it?

GIVING OUR TIME

If it is hard for us as businesspeople to give of our financial resources, it seems even harder to get a handle on giving our time. We can replace money, but most of us have learned to appreciate the importance and value of time in the business world. We fully recognize that time is irreplaceable and is our most valuable resource. There are 168 hours in a week, and most of us wish there were more. In fact, businesspeople tend to take fewer vacations, sleep less, and work longer hours than almost any other group of people on the planet. How, then, can we give our time?

Once we determine to give those hours to God's work, we will find, as many before us have, that we still manage to get all the important stuff done. I learned this lesson in a personal way several years ago when I felt God calling me to serve on the Texas State Board of Education, an unpaid, time-consuming job with tremendous responsibilities. You don't just juggle these new duties along with the multiple other tasks you normally accomplish in your profession. You must learn to listen to God as He shows you ways to increase your service and effectiveness to others.

"THE DOWN AND OUT"

Ann Platz, well-known Atlanta interior designer, author, and Christian speaker, years ago began using her talents to help certain widowed or divorced people return to life and hope. Quietly, without notice or fanfare, Ann would slip into a bare apartment or run-down house and take whatever was there and make it beautiful. She would spend a valuable Saturday helping people unpack boxes, clear out clutter, display keepsakes, and utilize their good linens, china, and artwork to beautify their home. Always, she placed a Bible on the bedside table and a rose in a vase beside it.

"God wants you to realize you are precious to Him," she told each of her amazed new clients, "and He sees you as worthy of His best." When Ann left each dwelling, it looked beautiful and welcoming. "You have made me feel like a queen," one woman told her.

Giving her time and energies to the brokenhearted became a unique mission field for Ann Platz—and it resulted in lives being restored. As the years passed, Ann moved into Christian speaking and mentoring, and then to writing many excellent Christian books. Her story illustrates that when we give of ourselves, our time, and our talents, God will lead us to new levels and methods of reaching His people. He will prosper our efforts.

THE NEXT GENERATION

Stephen W. Dement, founder and president of Landmark Title, Inc., in Tyler, Texas, actually works only half time at his continually growing business, where he oversees a staff of fifty. Mornings are devoted to teaching at a Christian school he founded in 1997. "I was only forty-three years old at the time, had no powerful community resources, certainly was no mover and shaker, and had no experience as an educator," Steve said. "People thought I was nuts."

Steve explained that his Bible study group had explored ways to help accomplish God's purposes. "God moved my heart to get into teaching from biblical precepts. In time, I knew I would do all I could to establish a new Christian school."

The amazing Brook Hill School story will be told in a later chapter. For now, though, consider that Steve Dement gives at least 50 percent of his working hours to God's work with youth. He teaches twelfth-grade government classes in the fall, economics classes each spring, and advanced classes in American history throughout the year.

How does he oversee his title company, which continues to prosper and grow? "If you pursue God's work and pursue it wholeheartedly, He will supplement your efforts," Steve says. "God literally sends people to you who can supply whatever you need."

BENEFITS OF STEWARDSHIP

"Here is a trustworthy saying: If anyone sets his heart on being an overseer, he desires a noble task" (1 Timothy 3:1, NIV). Understanding stewardship, for most of us, requires a paradigm shift in our thinking about finances and resources, along with an understanding of the value and potential within our natural and spiritual gifts and talents. These talents under God's direction can prove virtually limitless—if, that is, we undertake the ongoing task of learning and implementing God's precepts.

Interestingly, following God's guidance often reveals talents we didn't know we possessed. Steve Dement learned he could teach children and motivate them to love learning. Jackie Beavers discovered she could build an exceptionally successful and lucrative business from almost nothing, teaching housewives business from the Bible. "When God is our teacher, we don't expect to fail," she says.

As our stewardship skills increase and we manage whatever God gives us with wisdom and care, our vision for His kingdom increases exponentially. More and more, we come to see that everything that exists truly belongs to God. We are to manage well whatever He places under our authority; that mandate becomes our primary business. Whatever we engage in—whether a title company, bank, retail establishment, or law practice—our vocation serves as our means of obeying God and furthering His purposes.

SECTION THREE

LEADERSHIP

I will bless you [with abundant increase of favors] and
make your name famous and distinguished, and you
will be a blessing [dispensing good to others].
—Genesis 12:2 (AMP)

CHAPTER NINE

CALLED TO LEADERSHIP

God designed and equipped His people for leadership. Though strong leadership potential may exist in great numbers of us, very few respond to His highest call for our lives.

Why? For some, it's a lack of belief in the awesome power of God, which He makes available to our supposedly ordinary lives. For others, it might mean losing the approval of family or friends. And for all too many, it's the idea of allowing God to lead us into a community or national or worldwide leadership assignment too overwhelmingly costly to contemplate.

The stark fact is that God sees His man or His woman as someone He can equip, train, and send forth to do great exploits. Corporate managers expect record-breaking results from those they train and mentor. Skilled business trainers and managers can teach highly effective principles and techniques and even lead companies and corporations to make top-one-hundred status. What they cannot do, however, is convey limitless personal power into an individual life. Only God can do that.

God's magnificent vision for us is that we become nothing less than stewards, ambassadors, and leaders on earth. How many of us pray to grow into His vision for us?

QUESTION

Am I willing to grow into leadership? From God's perspective, that question is ancient and timeless. Picture Jesus as He walked along the Galilee shore, choosing men who would follow Him. The twelve He chose, those who for some reason left everything they had to follow Him, He made into leaders of men.

Those twelve rough, mostly untutored men apparently had little in the way of outstanding talents, education, or personal gifts. Jesus, however, could see into their hearts. He knew His small band of disciples was destined to become world-changers. To one of the most imperfect personalities in the group, Jesus said, "[T]hou art Peter, and upon this rock I will build my church" (Matthew 16:18, KJV). While the rock upon which the Lord's church would be built was the gospel of Christ, the Lord did use Peter in powerful ways during the early years of the church.

You and I, like Peter, may be rough, unpolished, impetuous, hot-tempered, argumentative, and even cowardly at times. History shows, however, that no man or woman created exists beyond the reach of Almighty God. In your life and mine, He can transform us, as He transformed the lives of James, Andrew, Mark, and the others who came to know Him intimately. Of the first twelve who followed Jesus, one chose to betray Him. The other eleven "ordinary" men became some of the mightiest and most lastingly effective leaders in recorded history.

BECOMING WILLING

God can wait. We may agitate, fluctuate, and vacillate, reluctant to answer His call on our lives. He walks with us as we learn to become His stewards, a precursor to leadership. He waits for us to listen and hear His voice. His Holy Spirit prompts us to stir up the gifts that are within us and gradually leads us into leadership.

At a revival meeting, an evangelist gave the following three altar calls: salvation, healing, and dedication of known and unknown talents to God.

That last plea drew dozens of men and women to the altar, weeping at the realization of how much they had withheld from Him.

"God, what do I have that You can use? I offer myself to You."

"Lord, here am I. Send me."

How often do we pray such prayers? How much of ourselves will we give to Him? Will I actually allow Him to enlarge my small life and the snug little world I have created for myself? Am I really willing to step out beyond my own self-constructed boundaries? Will I allow God to use me in His grand desire to change His world?

In any business environment, it is a given that successful men and women have to be willing to change, compete, and grow. In a God-led business, we must be willing to follow Christ into today's tough marketplace. We must be willing to seek God daily and *follow* His lead. Ultimately, we must be willing to accept leadership roles He opens for us, accept His Great Commission, and accept our opportunities to serve.

BECOMING A LEADER

At age forty-three, Stephen W. Dement, the founder and president of Landmark Title, surely did not see himself as a community leader. Though he headed his own growing title company and was a committed Christian who continually studied the things of God as he sought the Lord's direction for his life, Steve considered himself to be only a normal up-and-coming businessman with no particular leadership skills.

Other members of his Bible study group also were seeking to learn God's purposes for their lives and businesses. "That question surrounded us for some time," Steve remembers. "Individually and as a group, we did spend a significant amount of time praying about it."

In 1989 Steve became convinced that he was supposed to facilitate the founding of a school that would teach the precepts of God. Tyler, Texas, already had several Christian schools in the community. Why should another one be established? How does a non-educator found a school? Where does he begin, and how does he fund the operation?

"I had absolutely no idea," Steve Dement said. "I had no experience as an educator, was not a person of wealth, and knew none of our community's prominent movers and shakers."

Viewing the Dement assignment from a cold, practical business standpoint, most would conclude: no way. As a Spirit-led businessman, however, Dement simply asked, "How?"

"I learned that from the moment you say yes to God, He begins to send whatever you need to complete His plan," Steve says. "Land, money, advice, expertise, staff, assistance—whatever you need appears as you need it. He even sends people you don't know to help when you reach a crisis point."

Stephen Dement admits, of course, that establishing a school requires incredible amounts of effort, persistence, and prayer, and a continuing willingness to learn. It also requires a singleness of purpose that allows you to overlook the opinions of those who think you are nuts. But as God opened doors and supplied people, investors, donors, expertise, and so much more, Stephen also received superb leadership training. He was living and moving and building under the shadow of the Almighty as God built leadership, wisdom, and skills into his life.

God desires to build us up, and His method always has been simple, from the earth's beginning. "Call to Me, and I will answer you, and I will tell you great and mighty things, which you do not know" (Jeremiah 33:3, NASB).

Steve Dement describes the Brook Hill School in 1989 as a "field of dreams." He says no students or prospects were visible. But by word of mouth, students and contributors came. In 1997 there were 31 students in grades six through eight. Now, enrollment includes 525 students among all the grades, with a projected 950 pupils in the years to come. Tuition covers 80 percent of the operating expenses, and the rest comes from donations. The school's campus includes two hundred acres, and a student boarding program began in 2004. One of the school's graduates is now an engineer and teaches Sunday school. When he came to the school from Vietnam, that student had never even heard the name of Jesus Christ.

Leadership? Not only does Stephen W. Dement serve as president of the title company he founded, but he also has expanded his scope to include the office of chairman of the board of directors of the Brook Hill School. The fifteen-member board not only oversees the provision of thorough grounding in traditional coursework as taught from Christian precepts, but also offers students field trips in governmental and Christian mission efforts.

Steve Dement's "field of dreams" continues to grow and prosper. For more than twenty years, God has used his efforts to influence the lives of youngsters as he teaches them the love of learning and the rich benefits of seeking the truth.

COMMITMENT

By now, the astute reader has caught on to the process by which God creates business leaders. It's not so much a question of intellect and education, but rather a commitment to God and His purposes for one in His kingdom. Successful Christian businesspeople seem to find themselves to be a people who are committed to the following qualities:

- Obedience—in even the smallest acts of their business and personal life
- Prayerfulness—as they seek and listen to God
- Excellence—upholding Godly ethical standards in their business
- Sharing—their faith with others by example and speech
- Faith—in God and the belief that, with Him, all things are possible
- Courage—to follow His commandments
- Ability—to envision the great things they can accomplish with Him

This list can be expanded indefinitely. We can easily see that as God seeks the man or woman willing to be trained and used in leadership on His earth, He teaches that individual to renounce a lot of the world's ideas about leadership and take on the far more powerful precepts of holiness.

Does this sound like the marketplace you know? Consider that God has His people occupying judgeships, corporate boards, small businesses, retail shops, service industries, and every other public arena. Each person has a sphere of influence, a range of gifts and talents, and a heart and mind growing by stages into a more perfect love of God. Just begin to realize that this is where real ministry takes place. Not only do you and I have an opportunity to succeed financially in the business world, but with a willing desire to be committed to His purposes, we can succeed spiritually as well.

No Respecter of Persons

How do you rate your own leadership skills? How do you see your role in business in terms of leadership? How does God see it?

We usually do not see ourselves as God sees us. We often do not feel able or worthy of leadership or success. Many times our circumstances are such that we are so focused on survival we cannot or do not even think about God's plans. How many times have we been in a situation that seemed hopeless, only to later understand that it was all a part of His plan for us?

When the telephone industry diversified in the late 1980s, a young mid-level executive lost her job. At first Susan Speros felt totally bewildered and disconnected. Soon, however, she was consulting with business owners who needed telecommunications advice, working from a small home office.

Not long after, she hired technicians and began installing telephones and running cables for the increasing numbers of business computers being installed. She made herself knowledgeable about computers, installations, and a variety of long-distance telephone carriers, and she helped small businesses comparison-shop and wisely manage their computer and telecommunications investments. Most significantly, Susan decided that her company would serve its customers twenty-four hours a day. If a storm knocked out equipment, it would be repaired immediately. Thus her small company guaranteed service few larger corporations offered.

Susan's three companies today service businesses from coastal Georgia to North Carolina. Still in her forties, she enjoys professional respect, a healthy net worth, and community leadership. God's principle of not "being a respecter of persons" may be one of the most important keys to her success. Susan considers the smallest business client as important as the largest and serves accordingly. God has promoted her and her business into positions of true leadership.

GOD'S TIMING

The world often produces ways to jump-start us into prosperity, prominence, or promises of business success. True leaders, however, are seldom made overnight. A Hilton or a LeTourneau takes decades to come into leadership and industry dominance. Steve Dement's school, which started as one man's vision, has been built into something substantial through a slow, orderly process. Working alone in her bedroom, Susan Speros could not have imagined that her company trucks would one day travel the back roads and highways of coastal Georgia and the Carolinas.

By contrast, we all know businessmen and -women who, impatient for growth and profit, entered into a partnership or merger that later proved disastrous. One sign of Christian maturity is the ability to wait on God. It's a well-known business axiom that timing is everything. Many a Christian business owner or professional has discovered God's timing to be infallible, but to our minds, terribly slow. The message is this: Christian leadership usually does not happen overnight. Walk in God's path, however, and you choose a sure road to every sort of prosperity … no matter how long it takes or how small the start-up. Take my friend Eduardo, for example.

MARKETPLACE MINISTRY IN MEXICO

I met Eduardo on one of my trips to Mexico to speak to a gathering of Mexican businessmen and -women. His story touched my heart. In a small town where there seemed little commercial opportunity, Eduardo had been driving a bread truck for thirty-two years—a good job and a successful career. He had an entrepreneurial spirit, however, and saved money to start his own business.

After three decades Eduardo, now middle-aged, was able to buy equipment and become a street vendor of tacos, burritos, American hot dogs, and other locally popular food items. His business is led by God, Eduardo believes, and the businessman gives back so as to further kingdom work. Each Sunday night following church services, people swarm to his concession stand parked outside the church and stand in line to buy the hot, tasty food. Eduardo gives all Sunday-night profits, a sizable sum, to the church.

To the American used to high visibility and big deals, Eduardo's example of leadership and success might seem like small potatoes. But true leadership comes in various-sized packages from towns and provinces of all sizes. Remember those who, speaking of Jesus, asked, "Can any good come out of Nazareth?" (John 1:46, NKJV).

In the eyes of God, Eduardo's church and community leadership may well be as great as that attained by any man or woman who makes the evening news. Who knows the effectiveness of Eduardo's private mission field? Who can measure his business and personal success? Only God. Remember, He is training Eduardo and you and me for leadership, here and now. "Choose for yourselves this day whom you will serve ... But as for me and my household, we will serve the Lord" (Joshua 24:15, NIV). This is our key choice in preparation for leadership, good business, and lifelong success.

CHAPTER TEN

---◆◆◆---

MANAGEMENT KEYS

Those who own or manage a business obviously seek employees who will reflect the company's principles and standards as they conduct business on the company's behalf. God does the same. The people God uses are principled people. They are known as people of moral substance, men and women committed to doing exactly what God wants them to do, no matter the cost. They display an unusual level of leadership in upholding His principles.

As businesspeople, we can list certain business, moral, and ethical standards by which we operate; rules that work; rules we do not compromise. Most of us, however, may not have measured our business practices against our highest vision—that of serving as a trusted steward and an active ambassador for God.

LOOKING AHEAD

Few talented businesspeople need to be urged to plan ahead. We are competitive, forward-thinking types. I always have loved the saying, "Most people don't plan to fail ... they fail to plan." As businesspeople, we know how many residences we want to sell this year, how many franchise units we'll add in the next decade, what sales increases we intend to make this month, and so on. And if we're included among the supernaturally visionary few who operate via a business prayer plan, God may show us ideas and plans far bigger than those envisioned by other equally talented businesspeople.

Business leaders consider such mental projections fundamental to success. Napoleon Hill said that "what man can conceive and believe—he can achieve."

The Bible states it this way: "For as he thinks within himself, so he is" (Proverbs 23:7, NKJV). It's no wonder that Christian businesspeople who attain marketplace excellence are called "visionaries."

Two Georgia businessmen and visionaries illustrate the point. The late Allen Paulsen, as CEO of the Gulfstream Aircraft Corporation, once said that the moment his newest aircraft broke world records, he immediately began work on designs that would become superior to his present best. "Records are made to be broken," he observed. "The best thing you can produce can always be improved."

Two and three decades ago, developer Thomas Cousins created key structures that still define Atlanta's skyline. He said his habit of envisioning Atlanta's future needs inspired most of his projects. How far ahead did he plan? At least twenty years.

SONS OF ISSACHAR

Men and women led by God tend to see far ahead. They dream big and work hard to implement large goals. The world celebrates such people as business geniuses, which is undeniably true. Those of us who decide to seek God's vision for our particular career and life will surely tap into His immense and unlimited "genius." God can and will expand even an ordinary amount of talent and ability within the man or woman willing to follow Him and willing to do great exploits.

There was a famous group of visionaries and leaders in the Old Testament, the sons of Issachar. The Bible says that the sons of Issachar not only could look to and foresee the future, but also knew what to do about it. Due to their ability and willingness to act assertively, they became leaders during their day, so widely known they were written about in the Old Testament.

As Christian businesspeople, we have the ability and opportunity to be like the sons of Issachar. Doing so requires an alignment with the will of God and then the willingness to allow God to develop us as He desires. If willing, we can each become the leader that we were created and destined to become. We can impact lives and expand His kingdom, no matter where we are. Like Mr. Paulson and Mr. Cousins, we too can break records or meet the future needs of our surroundings.

THE COST

Things of great value always cost. Our salvation, freely given to us by God, cost Him dearly. However, even as we accept His priceless gift, we also must accept its costs. Taking a godly stand on certain public issues can make us a target for those who sling prejudice and hostility toward Christians. There may be times of sacrifice, misunderstanding, ridicule, or even persecution.

Such costs are overbalanced by certain priceless benefits: peace, joy, purpose, prosperity, God's promise of eternal life, and other gifts too numerous to list. Our courage and willingness to discipline ourselves in daily personal and business decisions, great and small, continually deepen our faith as we grow closer to God.

FOUR GODLY LEADERSHIP AND SUCCESS PRINCIPLES

I believe we must apply the following four principles to our lives as our foundation to personal and business success:

1. Excellence
2. Integrity
3. Good values
4. Wise counsel

Successful leadership and stewardship require commitment to those four principles. Without any one of those elements, we have no firm foundation from which to operate. These ancient foundational principles are time-tested. They work, but at times they may mean temporary sacrifice. They are principles you and I also must diligently work at in order to make them permanent in our lives.

1. EXCELLENCE

Excellence requires continuous commitment and discipline. As we strive to build a foundation of excellence in our business lives, we always will be challenged to sacrifice our commitment to excellence in order to solve a temporary problem. For example, the person who attends night school after work to study law intends to become a lawyer. His goal requires long hours of study and much sleep loss, but such discipline eventually brings significant rewards. So it is with building a foundation of excellence.

The benefits of committing to excellence in our business are twofold. First, we are pleasing to God and are a good example of Him in our life on this earth. Second, we gain recognition in the marketplace and have a reputation for excellence.

Following World War II, Japan's businesses were rebuilt by using a strategy of continuous improvement and striving toward excellence. Their commitment to excellence in the automobile manufacturing industry not only earned them a large share of the market, but also forced a higher standard of excellence upon the entire industry.

Another example is that of Benjamin Franklin, who sought to perfect certain virtues in his own character by a conscious aim toward excellence. Franklin kept daily records of his improvement in such traits as temperance, thrift, diligence, and good business practices. Even two hundred years after his death, we can easily recognize the impact that Mr. Franklin had on the United States and world government due to his individual excellence.

Excellent business practices should be a hallmark of any Christian, but some seem to believe they cannot better themselves. They see themselves as too undisciplined to attain any extraordinary success. They lack faith in themselves. They do not see themselves as examples of excellence. A thirty-six-year-old man who felt he was supposed to go to medical school and work as a physician became discouraged because all the other medical students were in their early twenties. He began to feel foolish for putting himself and his family through such great sacrifice. "In four years you'll be forty years old. You can be forty and be a doctor, or you can be forty and wish you were a doctor," someone advised him. Those wise words from a Christian friend encouraged the man to continue to work toward the goal God had placed in his heart. Of course, the answer to such self-doubt is God. He helps us with self-discipline. He helps us overcome our doubts, and He alone can lead us into a life of excellence.

When we provide goods or services to the public, it is incumbent upon us, as Christians, to do so with excellence. Interestingly enough, when we do so, not only do we please God, but we also often find ourselves in a position of extreme success in the business world.

WAL-MART STORES

Sam Walton, founder of the immensely successful Wal-Mart Stores, Inc. (Walmart), loved to visit his stores. Even at an age when most men no longer worked, Sam Walton would drive up to a Wal-Mart store in his old pickup and walk through the aisles, putting himself in the shoes of the customer. Mr. Walton disciplined himself to this and many other similar practices in order to ensure that the excellence he envisioned for all Walmart stores was present in each and every one.

To excel means to go beyond or above and to outdo or surpass. Excellence means the state or quality of excelling—superiority. As it says in Proverbs, "Do you see a man skilled in his work? He will serve before kings; he will not serve before obscure men" (Proverbs 22:29, NIV). A good business prayer plan includes, "Lead me into excellence in all I think and do."

2. INTEGRITY

The word *integrity* probably brings the image of someone's face to your mind—such as your father, teacher, mentor, or beloved grandmother.

The word means "uprightness of character, honesty."ˣ You do not need a dictionary definition if you recall a mother who marched her son back to face the shopkeeper with the candy he stole or the boss who truthfully admitted a costly mistake to his supervisor.

True integrity makes a deep impression on the observer. There can be no real excellence without integrity, because both require thoroughness, attention to service, accuracy, and truthfulness. The woman of integrity returns to the store when she discovers the grocer gave her too much change. The man of integrity is sometimes described as a person who "does business on a handshake." When you give your word, people should be able to count on it.

Integrity makes someone bend over backward to make a matter right. Sometimes it requires sacrifice; at times I have lost money on a contract in order to fulfill it after circumstances changed that were not the fault of the customer. It is better to take a monetary loss than to have our integrity tainted.

This is not to mean that we should allow ourselves to be taken advantage of; I believe both parties to an agreement should be held accountable. Christians are not called to be doormats, but leaders and good stewards.

THE GOLDEN RULE ... JC PENNEY

J. C. Penney, founder of the J. C. Penney Company, Inc. (JC Penney), was all about integrity. When he first founded his business, he called it the Golden Rule Store, so named after the biblical principle of "Do to others as you would have them do to you" (Luke 6:31, NIV). As a result of Mr. Penney's leadership and business practices, his organization grew to become a well-known institution in the United States.

In 1990, Mr. W. R. Howell, then chairman of the board of directors of the J. C. Penney Company, told the following story in a speech:

> Mr. Penney was on the board of directors of a bank in Florida during the Great Depression. He had nothing to do with the day-to-day running of the business, but his name and reputation

were instrumental in bringing in depositors. Well, like so many other financial institutions at the time, the bank folded and there was an outcry from depositors. Many could not understand how a bank associated with Mr. Penney could fail while he remained a multimillionaire. Mr. Penney was so anguished by the event that he used a large part of his personal fortune to pay the depositors what they had lost. He clearly was under no legal obligation to do so. He simply felt it was the right thing to do. That's the kind of person he was—and that's the kind of legacy he left. He never forgot that when you're a company that serves the public, what you are and how you conduct yourself become a part of your name and reputation.[xi]

INTEGRITY = ENJOYMENT

Our integrity should ensure that others will trust us and want to do business with us. I personally want people to be excited when I contact them. I want them to look forward to doing business with me. I want them to enjoy conducting business with me and enjoy the process. Such trust is earned by a commitment to excellence and integrity.

Choose good partners, associates, and clients; be quick to rectify your faults and errors; and avoid these common mind-sets: "Everybody else does it," "Nobody will know," "They owe it to me," and "It's the only way to get ahead."

Rest assured, problems will arise in business. It is how a person handles a problem that tells much about his or her integrity and character. I'll choose to do business with someone I know I can count on to be there, even when things go wrong and times get tough. If I can depend on someone to fight the fight with me, rather than resort to blame and abandonment, I can sleep at night. Again, how we handle the problems that arise in business tells the world much about the kind of men and women you and I are, and believe me, the world is watching.

3. VALUES

What is most important to you? Both God and man will judge you by your values. The ideas that you regard highly, the people you esteem, and your estimation of the tangible and intangible worth of things tell much about you.

What is most important to your business? When you answer that question fully, you have defined the scope of this book. If it is "your" business, it becomes exactly as complete and fulfilled as the rest of your life. If it is God's business, you may expect to see great things.

Here are some common things businesspeople value. Check those that apply to you:

- · People
- Money
- Reputation
- Achievement
- Sleep at night
- Comfort
- Family
- Peace of mind
- Faith in God
- Pleasure

From the above list you may form a rough sketch of the shape of your career or business thus far. Your values contribute much to your success or failure in business and in life.

A biblical perspective of values does not necessarily equate to the values we find in our world today. The things the Bible teaches us to value are pretty simple and easily prioritized:

- Our relationship with God
- Our relationship with our family
- Our relationships with other people

There are more scriptures in the Bible about money and finances than about any other subject, some two thousand. In addition, there are many proverbs and parables regarding business and business practices. But we must remember that the purpose of such scripture is to lead us into a better relationship with God, family, and fellow man. By putting God and people first, we always will find that we will receive a reward, whether it is financial success, family harmony, or simply the knowledge that we did what was right in the eyes of God.

I love what Walt Disney said: "When you do something so well that the customers not only come back, but they bring their friends, you are then truly successful in your endeavor."

A Young King

In 1 Kings 12, there is a story of a young man named Rehoboam, who became king of Israel upon the death of his father, Solomon. Once crowned, he was immediately confronted by citizens who were eager to know if he was going to be as hard a leader as his father had been. "Your father put a heavy yoke on us," they told him, "but now lighten the harsh labor and the heavy yoke he put on us, and we will serve you."

Rehoboam told them to come back in three days for an answer, and he consulted with the elders who had served his father. "How would you advise me to answer these people?" he asked. They replied, "If today you will be a servant to these people and serve them and give them a favorable answer, they will always be your servants."

Instead of listening to the wisdom of the elders, Rehoboam rejected their advice and consulted young men he had grown up with who were serving him. When he asked for their advice, they replied, "Tell these people who have said to you, 'Your father put a heavy yoke on us, but make our yoke lighter'—tell them, 'My little finger is thicker than my father's waist. My father laid on you a heavy yoke; I will make it even heavier. My father scourged you with whips; I will scourge you with scorpions.'"

Three days later, the king made a tremendous mistake by answering the Israelites as harshly as his friends had recommended. As might be expected, the people rebelled and refused to work for him. When King Rehoboam sent an overseer in charge of forced labor to the people, they stoned him to death, and Rehoboam himself barely escaped, fleeing on his chariot. The Bible tells us that "Israel has been in rebellion against the house of David to this day."

Young King Rehoboam did not place a high enough value on his people. His actions were clearly selfish and prideful. King Rehoboam chose to elevate himself and his new power over the people by force, rather than by wise leadership. The result was disastrous.

Our Employees

How do we lead our companies, our departments, our churches? Do we put people first? By putting people first and teaching them to recognize that the success of our endeavor will affect all, we can build loyalty to the organization through love rather than by demand.

I intentionally begin this process when interviewing prospective employees. I tell them that I do not expect them to work at my business for the rest of their life. "In fact," I usually say, "I probably will not run this business the rest of my life. However, as long as we are a part of the organization, we should do our best to make the company successful."

I then inform them that when their "season" with our company is over, they should share that fact with me. "Please do not give me a two-week notice," I say. "Talk to me as soon as you begin to realize that your time here is coming to an end. I will not feel betrayed and immediately fire you. In fact," I continue, "allow me to help you. I will pray with you, write letters of recommendation, and give you time off for interviews. All I ask during this process is that you continue to do your job, be honest with me at all times, and give me two or three *months'* notice so we can, together, find a replacement for you and train him or her."

I cannot tell you the looks of shock on most applicants' faces. Most have known only a workplace that is hard and demanding, and will possibly fire you the minute you become disloyal and want to leave. I do understand that some businesses cannot implement this particular practice, but I can assure you an alternative to the harsh manner in which most employees are treated during a transition can be found.

By the way, most of my employees stay with me for several years. When they leave, I typically receive two to three months' notice. The ability to take the proper time to replace and train someone who will become an important part of my business has proved to be a great advantage. When my employees leave, it is almost like a young family member separating to go on an adventure. We are sorrowful, yet excited at what God is going to do for that person in his or her life.

4. WISE COUNSEL

Every wise man and woman knows when and where to turn for wise counsel. We go to God in prayer, find His advice in His word, and meditate on the instructions He gives us.

Many times, however, we want human input. We need a "think tank" or even one other viewpoint. We are fortunate if our husband or wife is the one most in sync with our business goals and dreams. Otherwise, we must choose our consultants carefully.

Why do we seek human counsel? For one thing, there is wisdom in the experience of others. Counsel, or "consultation for exchange of advice and opinions,"[xii] can be valuable beyond price *if* we consult with godly mentors, elders, and expert advisors. If they do not share our Christian worldview, however, their advice could bring disastrous results.

From the godly elders we know, we can gain the benefits of long experience. Our family, our greatest asset, offers a wealth of wisdom. Wives and husbands love, encourage, and support us in our endeavors. As we live our lives together, their counsel becomes even stronger and more precious with each passing year. And how many times has our own small son or daughter said something so mature and sensible that we feel astonished?

Some are fortunate to have had parents who taught them good business practices as they were growing up. Some may even have had an opportunity to work in a family business. Susan Speros said her father, a hardworking entrepreneur who started several small businesses, regularly sat his wife and young children around the kitchen table, where he discussed his plans and listened to their input. "What I learned from this as a child gave me confidence as an adult that I could succeed in my own business," Susan said. My own father's business talents and methods often lie behind the success I achieve. I am grateful that he modeled good business practices before me in my young life.

We also can gain much excellent counsel from coworkers, employees, and customers if we allow our eyes to see and our ears to hear. The point is that we should stay alert for wise counsel from every source. God always sends us what we need. We may find the idea or advice we want in a book or in a news story, or we may hear it from the lips of a child.

We do *not* need advice from those who merely agree with us and who are at or below our own maturity level. This was Rehoboam's problem. He rejected the mature, wise counsel that had made his father successful, and he instead embraced self-serving, immature counsel from his friends. As the Bible says, "Whoever despises the work and counsel [of God] brings destruction upon himself, but he who [reverently] fears and respects the commandment [of God] is rewarded" (Proverbs 13:13, AMP).

ADVISORY BOARDS

I suggest that every business, large or small, establish an advisory board. While building an aviation business during the nineties, I found that an advisory board consisting of nonemployees and nonpartners became a strength to the organization that I could not foresee in the beginning. Many mistakes were prevented; several new ideas were generated. If you hold a leadership position in a small business or professional practice, I recommend that you create and implement an advisory board of successful men and women who have a relationship with God. These are people who can understand your spiritual position, yet know how to deal with the physical reality of the business world. My board never discussed budgets and finances; we addressed broader topics such as product quality, customer feedback, facility demands, etc. I have found that successful businesspeople are eager to help and would feel honored to be a part of your success.

Excellence, integrity, godly values, and *wise counsel* assist us in building a lifetime of business and personal success. Be sure to include your staff, employees, and partners in your commitment to these four principles. I believe that one plus one often equals three; in other words, unity lends a strength that cannot really be measured. The benefits of such unity are real.

ONE BUSINESSMAN'S STORY

In his book *It's Easier to Succeed Than to Fail* (1989), S. Truett Cathy, the megasuccessful businessman who founded and served as CEO of the Chick-fil-A company, tells of a time in 1982 when his famous chain fell on hard times. The company had expanded into several shopping malls that were slow to be completed, and the delays were costly. Interest rates had risen to 22 percent, and Cathy did not want to incur debt.

He decided to take his management staff to a quiet retreat spot where they could wrestle with several problems. As they talked things through, they saw no immediate answers, Cathy said. Then his son Dan, a real administrator, asked "Why are we in business? Why are we here? Why are we alive?"

His father admits he wanted to talk about *how*, not *why*. How they would turn a slumbering company around seemed to him to be the top priority on their agenda. Dan's questions at first seemed beside the point.

Nonetheless, the staff launched into deep discussion, and after honing their ideas for several hours, they decided on a two-point statement of corporate purpose.

1. To glorify God by being a faithful steward of all that is entrusted to us.
2. To have a positive influence on all who come in contact with Chick-fil-A.

Those simple statements formed the basis of all decisions made during the remainder of their problem-solving session, and the rest is history.

Truett Cathy's legendary success story is well known to most of the business world.

"One of my values is that I honor God by being a successful businessman," he wrote. "As a Christian, I think I can glorify God best by success and not by failure."

With a business based on excellence, integrity, good values, and wise counsel, success for any of us seems certain. As the apostle Paul wrote to the Romans, "If God is for us, who can be against us?" (Romans 8:31, NIV). Wise businesspeople remember that truth when discouragement hits. They assess their core values, gather their confidence in God, move forward in integrity, and look toward a future that promises all goodness and mercy.

CHAPTER ELEVEN

HEARING GOD'S VOICE

S o often Christian businesspeople get a great business idea and say, "God told me to do it." They go all-out, totally enthusiastic, but they don't do any homework … no research. They don't balance their ideas against God's written word, the Bible, nor do they seek counsel. Soon they are in trouble. It happens all the time.

It is critical for us to hear God if we are to experience all He has for us. Many of us, including myself, have been oblivious about the importance of hearing God's voice in our business. We believe we operate a "Christian enterprise" when, in truth, God is merely a *silent partner*. We pray, tell Him our plans and decisions, and assume He will bless them. It was some time before I learned He does not operate in that manner, nor should we.

The first time I heard God speak to me about business occurred soon after that humbling experience described in chapter one. I had been a Christian for a decade and had successfully founded and sold several small businesses. I was serious about Christianity and based my life on my faith and the Word, conducting my business on biblical principles. "God, I'm going here and doing such and such," I would pray. "Will You bless my steps?" That is how I operated my businesses during the first ten years of my Christian walk. Later, I would learn to ask Him *where* to step, rather than simply to *bless* my steps.

A SECRET LEARNED

Several months after that roadside experience, my wife and I found ourselves considering a move … possibly to Tyler, Texas, to seek new business opportunities. Prior to that trip, everything had dried up for me, it seemed. For long months, nothing I had tried in business seemed to work. I had written business plan after business plan, realizing as I worked on them that this was not God's plan for me. However, I did not know what else to do. By now I felt convinced I should find a job instead of attempting another entrepreneurial start-up. As we drove toward Tyler for an interview with a local businessman, my wife, son, and daughter fell asleep. During the now quiet drive, a thought occurred to me, and I found myself asking, "What would it take to establish an aviation school in Tyler?"

My former partners and I had considered locating an aviation business in Tyler a few years prior but had dropped the idea. During the next hour's drive to our destination, a business plan began to form in my mind. It grew, steadily and effortlessly, as if I was receiving a computer-like information download.

As we approached the city of Tyler, Shannon, Courtney, and Matthew woke up, and I put all my new ideas aside. We checked into our hotel, and I swam with the kids in the swimming pool, went to bed early, and got up for my seven o'clock meeting the next morning.

Intending to speak of business opportunities in the area in a general manner, I was quite surprised when the first thing the businessman with whom I was meeting asked, "What would it take to start a flight school in Tyler?" Interestingly enough, I had the plan.

I laid it out, and four months later we opened the school. Even then, I did not recognize God's role in our circumstances. It seemed like a coincidence that I'd had that mental exercise during the drive to Tyler, and then got hit with the flight school question. *Pretty lucky*, I thought.

One of my first and most important tasks at the new aviation school was to hire the chief flight instructor, who had to have very specific qualifications. Someone advised me to approach the retired chief flight instructor and director of aviation at LeTourneau University, located in nearby Longview, Texas. The gentleman was currently a Federal Aviation Administration (FAA) examiner, considered one of the best in his field. After a lunch meeting, I wanted to hire the man. I knew he would be incredible, but he was out of my league. He was worth much more money than my new company could afford to pay him.

Instead, I hired another highly qualified person who seemed like a good fit, yet after only a couple of weeks, I knew something wasn't right. I prayed about it and then phoned a gentleman I had met after moving to Tyler. He was a successful, prominent business leader, someone I had met in church and come to respect in a short period of time. The man was different from others. He seemed to operate his business in a manner slightly different from the norm. I needed advice but was too new in town to know anyone else to call.

He must have wondered why I asked him to lunch. No doubt he thought I was in trouble with my new venture, and he probably was relieved when I finally got around to telling him what was bothering me. My questions to him were, "Does God desire to be involved in the day-to-day activities of our businesses on this earth? Does He want to be a part of the decision-making process? Can He and will He communicate His desires for 'His' business?" You see, I had realized that this business and everything else on the earth belongs to God. For me to make all the decisions myself, without consulting the "owner," did not seem right.

"Randy," said this extremely successful businessman, "let me tell you a secret—the secret to my success. I don't make a business decision without asking the Lord and hearing His answer." He told me, "You are thirty-six years old. You don't have time to waste. You need to put every business question before the Lord, listen for His answer, and then follow His instructions."

I left that meeting with a heavy heart, realizing that I *had* heard God regarding the chief flight instructor position but had not acted. *You should have hired that other guy,* I told myself. *God put him on your heart, and He would have made a way.*

At home, I went into my prayer closet and repented. "Lord, do I have to fire someone because of my mistake?" I prayed. "This person moved here for the job. It doesn't seem right." I felt heavyhearted at the thought of the mistake I'd made and the possible ramifications. How in the world could I make it right?

I couldn't correct the situation, but God could. Within a week, our chief flight instructor received an unexpected job offer from a university in another state, an offer too good to refuse. I had not even mentioned anything to this person, but was amazed at how God took care of the entire situation.

I went back to my first choice for the chief flight instructor, the man so highly respected by the FAA and the entire aviation community in our region, and I simply told him the truth. He is a Christian, and his reply was, "Randy, I'm not really interested in a big salary. What I'd really like is an opportunity to earn some ownership in your business. I believe in what you are doing, and I believe we can impact lives."

"I am sure we will be able to accomplish that," I assured him. During the next eleven years, J. C. Harder and I worked together, and we did impact lives.

GOD SPEAKS

Through that experience, I learned that God wants to speak to us. I saw that the idea that had popped into my mind during the drive to Tyler, the businessman's query about starting an aviation school, and my strong desire to hire a particular man for an important job were God's methods of speaking to me. Not any of these events were random! I needed to learn how to know when God was speaking, nudging, or confronting me.

Jesus said, "My sheep listen to my voice" (John 10:27, NIV). I saw I needed to recognize His voice at all times and in all circumstances. This was the first time I had "heard" the Lord instruct me about my business. Believe me, it got my attention.

Yes, God really does speak to us about business. The Bible tells us He is interested in every detail of our life, and that would surely include our business life. The keys are expectation and trust—"expectation" that He will answer us and "trust" that His answer is correct. I believe that God will always answer our sincere questions. We may not always like the answer, but it is there for us. Finding His answer is up to us. We must learn to listen to God speak in the many, many ways that He does.

HEARING HIM

From the beginning, God has desired to speak to man. He communicated with Adam, Cain, Noah, Abraham, David, and just about every other man and woman the Bible records. He spoke to Moses and gave us the Ten Commandments. He spoke to Jesus, and through Him, gave us our salvation. I believe He has spoken to every man, woman, and child ever created, and He yearns for us to hear Him and respond to Him.

But how do we hear Him? The answer is really simple. We must listen. We must learn to listen for God's voice as we read scriptures, as we pray, as we think, and as we ask. We must learn to recognize God's hand in our situation, whether it is through circumstances, or words and actions of others. We can no more limit God's ability to communicate with us than we can limit God in any other manner. We tend to limit Him according to our ability to conceive and reason. We must remember that He is our Creator and He can communicate with us however He desires.

ONE RULE

As we look to God for answers and direction in our lives, we must make sure that the answers and the direction we think we are getting *always* line up with the Bible. God does not contradict Himself. His written word is for us to study, to learn, and to use as a measuring stick for our lives. We have the ability and blessing to compare what we believe we are hearing to the Bible. God will not "tell" you or me to do something that is not scriptural.

We also have the ability to pray about what we believe God is saying to us. When I pray, I ask God not only to give me direction but also to confirm within my spirit the things I believe I am hearing.

We must remember that we are only humans—logical and emotional beings that make mistakes. I have found that by comparing what I am hearing with the written word of God and asking Him for confirmation in prayer, I have been able to avoid many mistakes and to become more accurate in my communication with God. He is a communicator and will use anything from a donkey to His Son on the cross to communicate with us.

I cannot tell you how many times in my life I have sought the Lord for a decision and after spending time in prayer, I knew exactly what needed to be done and how to do it. Sometimes, the answer and instructions I would get from Him did not reflect the "normal" way for dealing with that particular issue. However, I always have found it to be the "right" way.

A Comeback

A man who owned three businesses told what happened after two of his sons went to war. Each young man had managed one of the father's businesses, and the man now was struggling to find managers who could replace his sons. As the months dragged on, the businessman found himself stretched to the limit, and all three businesses began to flounder.

None of this mattered much to the businessman and his wife, however, as they prayed for their boys' safety. After a year, the businessman had lost first one business, and then the second, and his own business had gone downhill. He found himself distraught with fear, overwork, and monetary loss. He dreaded the possibility of losing one son or both in the war. He even dreaded their safe return, because they would find their businesses gone.

In that state of hopelessness, the man threw himself on God, pleading for his sons' protection and asking Him how he could save his own store. God gave him a strange instruction.

"I got the feeling I should paint the place and spruce it up," the man said. "That made no sense, unless I was going to have to sell the business.

But I kept getting the same message, so I bought some paint and started to work."

As the man was freshening the interior of his store, he found his spirits lifting. He did the work himself, and as he worked, memories of beginning his business surfaced, and he found himself realizing how God had been with him for twenty-five years, had prospered him, and had given him two fine sons and a good wife.

One morning, his despair simply vanished, and the store looked prosperous. Business picked up. A few months later, his soldier sons came home and the family rejoiced. The boys helped their father rebuild his struggling store, and within five years that store again had two new branches, bigger and better this time.

Was God involved in all this? "Yes," the man replied without hesitation. "The amazing thing is that my comeback began after I heard Him tell me to roll up my sleeves and paint that old store."

WRITTEN INSTRUCTIONS

God speaks to us through the logos, His written word. "All scripture is given to us," the apostle Paul wrote to Timothy, "by inspiration of God, and is profitable for doctrine, for reproof, for correction, for instruction in righteousness; that the man of God may be complete, thoroughly equipped for every good work" (2 Timothy 3:16–17, NKJV).

In all times and circumstances, scripture speaks to us. Wherever we choose to read among the sixty-six books of the Bible, God speaks to us. This is the book that exhorts us to get wisdom and understanding, and it is the only real road to that wisdom and understanding.

Evangelist Billy Graham has recommended a particular reading discipline. Read five Psalms and one chapter of Proverbs each morning, he advises, and read other portions of scripture at bedtime. The book of Psalms leads us to worship God. Pastor Dietrich Bonhoeffer, the German theologian who was executed by the Nazis during World War II, called Psalms "the prayer book of the Bible." Here are songs of courage, faith, and men's offering of worship and glory to God.

Proverbs, easy to understand and remember, are nuggets of wisdom we should apply to business and to life. It's surprising how often something we read in Proverbs or Psalms speaks directly to our present need.

An insurance salesman was awaiting two commission checks, and his funds were dwindling. He had a bill he needed to pay and was considering telephoning the company to say his payment would be late. That morning he read in Proverbs 3:27: "Do not withhold good from those to whom it is due, when it is in your power to act." Astounded at that specific direction, he also read verse 28: "Do not say to your neighbor, 'Come back tomorrow and I'll give it to you'—when you already have it with you." The man realized those were God's clear instructions to him at that moment. He wrote a check from the last of his funds to pay that bill, mailed it, and resolved not to worry. Later that same day, he received his two long-awaited commission checks in the mail.

God speaks to us personally, directly, and clearly through his written word. Don't leave home without it.

THE RHEMA WORD

The rhema word, as in the story above, is when a scripture passage comes alive to us at this present moment. It leaps to life *now*. Maybe it is a scripture we have read or heard preached a hundred times, but it means something to us now, today, that it never has meant before. The rhema word of God was what I was missing during those early years of my business life. I was making every effort to build my life around the logos word, but almost completely lacked the rhema word.

Rhema—hearing God speak to us in our present state—is what we businesspeople need to seek. *However*, this word must always be consistent with the logos word. For example, the logos word tells us that God will give us the desires of our heart. We might tell ourselves, therefore, that it's okay to desire a certain person to whom we are not married, and that God has given us love for him or her. This could not actually be a word from God, because it is written, "Thou shalt not commit adultery" (Exodus 20:14, KJV).

A strong word, therefore, always must line up with scripture. The rhema word you hear—the strong voice of God sounding in your heart—absolutely must be measured against His written authority to be sure it is true. Logos and rhema never contradict one another.

Therefore, know the logos word and seek to hear God through His rhema word. Arm yourself and your business with what the Bible calls "the sword of the spirit, which is the word of God" (Ephesians 6:17, NKJV).

PRAYER AND LISTENING

Remember, we are called to be priests. We *can* hear God speak. Through prayer, God communicates with us, if we allow Him. Over the years, I have discovered that prayer is far more than a one-way conversation. Conversation is a two-way deal. We must allow time for God to speak to us. We should listen and give Him time to answer when we call out to Him.

John D. Rockefeller, the nineteenth-century oil baron, was a shrewd businessman. His methods of business are not anything that I would want to emulate, but he did know the value of listening. A favorite little rhyme he liked to recite from memory went like this:

A wise old owl lived in an oak;
The more he saw the less he spoke.
The less he spoke, the more he heard.
Why aren't we all like that old bird?[xiii]

Perhaps we all should try to be like that little old owl when we communicate with our God. I have found that I have a tendency to do a lot of the talking during my prayer time, and I don't always quiet myself and listen as I should. I often want to simply recite my questions and problems to Him, not waiting for the answers I seek.

When you do take the time to listen, God can drop divine revelation into your spirit and mind. He revealed important things to me years ago during that fateful drive to Tyler with my family, seeking my next career opportunity. I didn't recognize those "thoughts" as being from God at the time, but looking back a year later, I could see the amazing path God had me on, beginning with that short automobile trip.

Sometimes we hear things from God that do not seem to match our circumstances. Years ago my editor friend Charlotte said she felt that God had told her more than once to renew her passport and hurry to complete a book she was writing. "I didn't get the passport, because I had no plans to leave the country," she said. "As for the book, I had all summer to complete it and wanted to do a careful job. I took my time with the project and turned it in just before the September deadline."

Meanwhile, however, a visiting missionary who spoke at Charlotte's church met her and invited her to make a short trip to South America to get acquainted with mission work there. "I felt sick," Charlotte said. "I never realized I had indeed heard God, and because I thought His message didn't meet my circumstances at the time, I didn't act. Because I had no current passport and had not completed my work, I had to pass up a great opportunity."

Later she told a pastor about her "wasted" opportunity. "I wouldn't call it wasted," he said. "I'm sure it taught you to move quickly when God speaks to you. You will never forget that lesson, I'm sure."

BE STILL AND KNOW

"Be still and know that I am God," He has told us (Psalm 46:10, NIV). We all know that command, but at times we simply live in such a whirlwind we can't seem to find a moment of quiet. We hardly find time for meaningful prayer, much less time to meditate on Proverbs or any other portion of scripture. It's ironic that the very disciplines that bring order to our chaotic lives are often the first things we dispense with when we are tired and hurried. We are like Lord Ashley, before he charged into battle, who prayed, "Oh, Lord. Thou knowest how busy I must be this day; if I forget thee, do not thou forget me."

We must make time and space to communicate with God, if we truly want to hear His voice. As someone once said, "If you would have God hear you when you pray, you must hear Him when He speaks."

HEARING GOD SPEAK IN THE MARKETPLACE

When we pray about a business matter and can't seem to hear an answer, are we praying incorrectly? Not necessarily. Sometimes God speaks to us through circumstances, or through other people. God certainly spoke to me through the words of the godly man I consulted when I was experiencing staffing problems at our flight school. Many times He speaks to us through a friend, business associate, or even a stranger, and especially through a spouse.

Other times, circumstances develop in such an amazing way that we feel certain it is "a God thing." In our elation, we may move forward too rapidly. People and circumstances certainly can speak God's will toward us on many occasions; however, we must remember that we can hear God and must check out such happenings with Him.

Questions to ask ourselves are: Do the circumstances line up with His word? Do they produce peace in my spirit?

God is in the center of the marketplace. He can speak in countless creative ways to make us hear Him and allow us to know when He speaks. I usually pray, "Lord, this was said, or that happened. What do you think? You know the truth. Please talk to me."

He does and He will.

YOUR BUSINESS PRAYER PLAN

Most entrepreneurs and businesspeople know the value of working out a business plan, but how many Christian businesspeople form a prayer plan for their businesses? Here are some suggestions:

- Find a quiet place and adequate time to plot prayer strategies for your career or business.
- Resolve to have a "hearing ear"; give yourself time to listen.
- Pray strategically. List your visions and objectives.
- Pray in advance, asking God to provide answers when you need them. Listen for them even in times of stress and pressure.
- Pray for discernment.

Once you set your business prayer plan into action, it is good to record the results. One woman decided to keep a prayer journal for one year, noting and recording every prayer she prayed. As she listened and saw answers, she recorded dates when prayers were answered. "I did this faithfully for a year," she said, "but did not renew my efforts the following year. Flipping through my journal, I could see very few prayer requests unanswered or problems left unsolved. I was convinced and amazed by God's faithfulness."

BENEFITS OF HEARING GOD'S VOICE

Not only your business, but God's (kingdom expansion) business will benefit from your listening for His timely instructions. You can expect to receive these benefits according to Christian International Business Network's Basic Biblical Business Course:

- *Encouragement* where these was discouragement or even despair
- *Peace* instead of turmoil
- *Understanding* replacing frustration
- *Hope* instead of thoughts of failure
- *Faith* where there is fear or doubt
- *Praise and thanksgiving* instead of complaints
- *Direction* where there was confusion
- *Success* rather than failure

ALLOWING GOD TO SPEAK INTO OUR BUSINESSES

Why, then, must we learn to listen to God's voice in our marketplace mission? John Wesley said, "The world is my pulpit." For us, the business world is our mission field. Within our business territory, great or small, God has appointed to each of us some astounding opportunities.

- We are to prosper not only for ourselves but also for the generations after us.
- We are to steward His earth.
- We are to be a blessing to others.
- And most of all, we are to minister His gospel.

He has entrusted this generation of businessmen and -women with enormous opportunities and awesome potential for success. As we said before, *every success in the Bible was based on a man or woman of God hearing the word of the Lord and acting upon that word.*

Let us learn to hear God's voice and be bold enough to act upon what we hear.

Chapter Twelve

Failure ... the Risk of Adventure

Throughout this book we have discussed the importance of recognizing our spiritual role within the business world, accepting that role, and pursuing all that God has for us to do and achieve on this earth. Just as the biblical stories of men and women pursuing the unreachable for God inspire awe, so do the stories of many other businessmen and -women who are alive today. The Spirit of God continues to direct His stewards and ambassadors in multiple, far-reaching ways. His influences are global, and our opportunities seem limitless.

One factor in stories of accomplishments like those of a Conrad Hilton, Stephen Dement, or Eduardo with his Mexican fast-food cart is that of adventure. Entrepreneurs constantly seem to ask themselves "What if—?" and Christian visionaries, in my opinion, seem to enjoy far more adventure and excitement than others.

We have, thus far, looked at several men and women who undertook such an adventure with God within their own workplace or business. All of these examples have ended with clear and resounding success. However, in reality not all adventures for God turn out as we might expect.

I would like to look at three examples of individuals who were fully committed to pursuing an adventure they believed to be from God. However, the results were not always good—at least in their eyes.

KING DAVID

King David of the Old Testament is one of my favorite biblical characters. He was a warrior, a nation builder, and a worshipper of God. His life really wasn't much different from our lives, if you really think about it. Those of us who undertake the challenge of building a business will experience many of the same challenges and trials that King David did. We also will taste the sweetness of victory and the bitterness of defeat.

When King David was very old and nearing the end of his life, he was literally run out of town by an adult son who wanted to become king. As David and his followers escaped Jerusalem, an old enemy chided the king and threw rocks at him. One of King David's men wanted to execute the rock thrower, but the king would not allow it. David felt that if he was no longer worthy to serve as king, then the man was right to throw rocks at him. In fact, King David spoke to God in prayer stating that if his time as king was at an end, then he would gladly relinquish all power to the next king. Even in defeat, King David turned to God with trust.

DR. BILL HAMMOND

Even as a young man, Bill Hammond knew he was called to preach and teach the world about God and His Son, Jesus. He has dedicated his life to that work and, like King David, has had both mountaintop experiences and hard times.

He tells the story of an experience he and his wife had many years ago. As a part of his ministry, Dr. Hammond felt led to purchase a piece of real estate in Arizona. The property was zoned for commercial use and could have been a perfect place for his school. You see, he and his wife felt that they were to create a school for pastors and laypeople that would equip their students for ministry and then send them out into the world.

The price for the property was $100,000, quite a large sum thirty years ago. He was able to raise one-half of the purchase price as a deposit, with a promise to pay the remaining $50,000 within twelve months. It has been said that the easiest way to make a year pass quickly is to have a note calling for a twelve-month balloon payment! Sure enough, the one-year time period came and went, and Dr. Hammond and his wife were not able to raise the balance due. Not only did they lose the commercial lot, but they also lost the original $50,000 they had placed as a down payment on the purchase.

Both Dr. Hammond and his wife felt grief at the foreclosure of their property. "After all these years in ministry, Bill, when are things going to level out?" she cried to her husband.

Dr. Hammond thought about his wife's question for a moment and then responded, "Never." He wisely understood that as long as they were on this earth, working and striving to expand the kingdom of God, they would be in constant battle with the spiritual and economic forces of the world.

RANDY AND SHANNON STEVENSON

THE ARCADIA

Several years ago, my wife, Shannon, and I began to sense the need for a facility that Christian speakers could come to in our small city, a neutral space not connected to any church or denomination, a place that would attract all generations and all types of people. We were excited to see what the Lord had in mind, and we began the process of finding out what that might be.

As time passed, Shannon and I agreed that this was our assignment, one that we had no idea how to complete. We prayed, we drove around town looking at buildings, and we kept our eyes and minds open to what He might show us. Others joined us in prayer, and together we waited.

Months went by. Then, one morning on our way downtown to vote, we both spotted a building on the square near our polling place. It was the old Arcadia Theatre, and a "For Sale" sign was taped to the front door. The theater was locked, but we peered through the windows to try to get a glimpse of what it was like inside. We decided to contact the owner, schedule a visit, and check things out further.

The minute we stepped into the lobby, both Shannon and I felt like this was what we had been watching and waiting for. We both simply "knew" this was it. The building was originally built in 1887 and was remodeled after a fire in 1925. It had been empty for years and needed a lot of work. The asking price was high considering its condition, but we didn't let that discourage us. After much prayer and deliberation, we decided to take a step of faith and make an offer of half the asking price, contingent upon the building's soundness.

To our surprise, the Lord gave us favor with the woman who owned the theater. She was touched by our vision of bringing Christian speakers and musicians to the city for our community. We even became friends with her through the process. When she accepted our offer, we were thrilled.

RESTORATION

With the financial backing and "partnership" of several Christian friends and family who believed in and supported our vision for such a center, we began restoring the old Arcadia Theatre in January 2005. Six months later it opened. The Arcadia originally had been designed for vaudeville shows, with a full stage, imposing columns, and ornate moldings. The old pipe organ was gone, but the structure itself remained in surprisingly good shape. The interior, however, needed much work.

Shannon enjoys retro décor, and the theater came alive under her touch. With its black awning and neon lights outside, the entrance attracted people from all over the square. Initially, we turned the theater lobby into a modern coffeehouse and lunch spot, and we had plans to update the larger theater area for hosting speakers and other events when we could. The plan was to allow the profits from the café to fund the restoration of the main theater area.

DEFICITS

The coffeehouse came alive with people and activity. However, rather than generating a profit from the café, we ran into deficits month after month.

As Shannon and I continued to pour money into the project, we began to see our plans to restore the main theater area slipping away. I didn't understand why this was happening and really wrestled with God over it. After all, we had done our research, had written a thorough business plan, and had a ministry plan in hand for this place. We are not quitters, and I could not accept this failure to complete the vision. Neither quitting nor failing was an option for me.

After two years, however, we reluctantly closed the café. While a great deal of ministry had taken place during those two years, the bottom line was that Shannon and I could not afford to keep the place open and fund the monthly deficits. However, we did still hold on to the original dream and vision for the building and believed that at some date in the future we would be able to tackle the project once again.

Closing the Arcadia was an embarrassment to me in a personal way. I felt that I had let everyone down, including God. I couldn't understand how this could have happened! We had done our homework and met our budgets, but the café simply couldn't maintain itself. This was a high-profile project in our community, and several of our friends had contributed to the project. What was I to say? What could I say? I was baffled. This was new territory for me; after all, I had operated several successful businesses in my career, and I certainly should have known what I was doing by now. How could I have allowed this to happen?

DISASTER

Then disaster really hit. One night in February 2009, we received a call that the downtown square was on fire. We were told that the fire had started in another historic building two structures down from the old Arcadia Theatre. We watched that night as the fire completely destroyed two historic buildings and severely damaged our theater. It was as if the financial failure of the venture was not enough—the destructive fire seemed like an exclamation mark at the end of an important statement.

FAILURE OR SUCCESS?

As we read these stories of King David, Dr. Hammond, and the Arcadia, it would be natural to assume that the sagas all ended in failure. We often are quick to judge the stories of others and to judge ourselves as failures when our expectations of positive outcomes are not fulfilled.

However, we must ask ourselves: what is failure? Did King David really fail? Was his leadership lacking? How about Dr. and Mrs. Hammond? Were they wrong to pursue the vision of the school and the purchase of the land? And finally, what about the Arcadia experience? Were Shannon and I and our friends wrong to pursue the vision for the Arcadia Theatre to become a center of ministry? Are all of these examples of failure?

I think not. From the world's perspective, perhaps they might be called failures because the individuals did not fully accomplish their own vision of their project. However, the real question is, "Were they failures in the eyes of God?"

We can look to the Bible for an answer to that question. Many of us know the wonderful and oft-quoted verse found in the Old Testament: "For I know the plans I have for you, declares the Lord. Plans to prosper you and not to harm you, plans to give you hope and a future" (Jeremiah 29:11, NIV).

JEREMIAH

The story of Jeremiah, though, is one of the saddest stories in the Bible. As a prophet called by God, Jeremiah delivers his message to the people of Judah—God's people—that they must turn from their ways, or they will be destroyed. They repeatedly reject him; among other things, they beat him and throw him into a pit to die. God keeps telling Jeremiah to deliver the message, and the people persist in rejecting it (and him), until finally the destruction warned of comes about—Jerusalem falls, and they are dragged off to Babylon in captivity.

Jeremiah's faith wavers; the book of Lamentations is his weeping lament over what he perceives as his failure. They didn't listen. Ever. Maybe he didn't get the message across. Maybe he misunderstood God's calling. Whatever the cause, he failed. Not exactly what most would call plans for "hope and a future."

Jeremiah is at times angry with God, at times despairing, and yet he ultimately comes to this conclusion—God is God, and whatever our understanding of His plans, He is worthy to be praised. Near the end of Lamentations, Jeremiah writes, "You, Lord, reign forever—Your throne endures from generation to generation." (Lamentations 5:19, NIV)

Jeremiah may have felt the emotions and experienced the self-condemning thoughts of failure because he did not see the results he expected to see, but to the contrary, he actually was successful due to his obedience to God's call. He was the opposite of a failure; he withstood persecution, temptation, heartache, loneliness, despair, and grief, and then repeatedly faced it all again to continue to fulfill the mission God had charged him with, even in the face of defeat. His story, if we read it from God's perspective, is not one of failure, but one of resounding success. And in this context, we can better understand the "hope and a future" that God has for him—perhaps not on this Earth, but an eternity of reward for a good and faithful servant.

BATTLES LOST, WARS WON

Just as Jeremiah was not a failure, neither was King David. In fact, he was restored to his kingship within a matter of days and continued to serve as king until his death.

Dr. Hammond and his wife did eventually build their school for the Lord. Christian International Ministry has a beautiful campus on the Florida coast where they have trained and equipped thousands of pastors and laypeople for a life of service.

And finally, Shannon and I have come to the conclusion that whatever happens to the historic Arcadia Theatre—whether it is used again for ministry or not—we and the others involved were obedient. In attempting to follow God's lead, we can never fully know the end results of our endeavors. I must admit, though, that it is our hope that the theater will someday be fully restored and used for His redemptive work.

ASSUMING THE RISK OF FAILURE

"You must go out on a limb to get to the fruit," is a simple saying that explains risk. Picture yourself perched on a strong branch close to the trunk of a tree. You want the fruit that hangs off the end of the limb, but to get to it you must let go of the tree trunk and climb out onto the weaker part of the limb. There is a risk that the limb may break under your weight.

Many want the fruits of success, but few are willing to take the chance of failure in order to obtain those fruits. When God calls us out on a limb, we must totally trust Him to protect us as we let go of safety to pursue whatever He has called us to do.

In addition to risk, we also must understand that we will encounter obstacles and hardships in undertaking the challenges and adventures that God has placed before us, whether in a new business or in a ministry. We even may fall off that limb and get beat up a little!

We also must realize that as we follow God into new adventures, we could be deemed a "failure" from the world's perspective (even from our own, if our standards are not God's), yet still be a "success" from a heavenly perspective.

PRESIDENT ADAMS

John Quincy Adams, the sixth president of the United States of America and son of the second president of the United States, continued to serve his country long after he concluded his presidency. Most Americans are not aware that he served in the US House of Representatives for seventeen years following his service as president, relentlessly working for solutions to many of the issues faced by our still-young nation.

The question of slavery was extremely important to Mr. Adams. In fact, every Monday for almost two decades, Mr. Adams raised the question of the legitimacy of slavery before the House. Every Monday he was dismissed. His persistence became irritating to many, so much so that the "gag rule" was enacted to prevent him from raising the controversial issue. Many took him for an old fool.

A reporter once asked him why he continued to raise the issue of slavery even though he failed time and time again to get Congress to address the question. Mr. Adams responded, "The duty is mine. The results are God's."

Mr. Adams understood that while he did fail to bring the issue of slavery to the floor of the House, he was successful in the eyes of God because he diligently and dutifully continued each Monday despite the world's opposition.

GOD'S CREATIONS

Using ordinary men and women, God can build something the size of a street vendor's business, a Christian school, a worldwide hotel chain, or any number of other ventures that meet physical and spiritual needs. We businessmen and businesswomen, as stewards for God, can achieve great and successful exploits for God. We can dream big dreams, envision huge plans, and build God's kingdom here on earth, brick upon brick, prayer upon prayer, as He gives the inspiration and the power. And we can grow big ourselves through experiencing failures and setbacks, because we know that "all things work together for those who love God and are called according to His purpose" (Romans 8:28, NIV).

Today's business world literally encompasses the earth. The marketplace offers more scope and far-reaching opportunities for ministry than ever before in the world's history. One thing has not changed, however. As Jesus said, "The harvest is plentiful but the workers are few" (Matthew 9:37, NASB).

I pray that all of us called to business may labor for the kingdom of God, knowing that His rewards will be eternal and beyond all price. I pray that each person reading these words will be challenged to undertake an adventure that could prove to be exciting and fulfilling.

Listen to His voice and step into your destiny!

THE VOICE OF ADVENTURE

**Those who try to keep their lives will lose them. But
those who give up their lives will save them.**

—Luke 17:33

There is a rawness and a wonder to life. Pursue it. Hunt for
it. Sell out to get it. Don't listen to the whines of those who have
settled for a second-rate life and want you to do the same so they
won't feel guilty. Your goal is not to live long; it's to live.

Jesus says the options are clear. On one side is the voice of
safety. You can build a fire in the hearth, stay inside, and stay
warm and dry and safe …

Or you can hear the voice of adventure—God's adventure.
Instead of building a fire in your hearth, build a fire in your heart.
Follow God's impulses. Adopt the child. Move overseas. Teach the
class. Change careers. Run for office. Make a difference. Sure, it
isn't safe, but what is?[xiv]

May God bless and prosper you in your ventures.

In Conclusion

In 1991 my grandfather, R. T. Stevenson, lay on his deathbed. My sister Karen and I happened to be at his side when he became coherent enough to speak. He looked at me and said, "I just hope my work is completed." At eighty-eight years old, my grandfather still farmed and was a partner in a hay-baling business. In fact, he was on the job with his partner of almost fifty years when he discovered the cancerous lump in his abdominal area. *Is he worried about completing a hay-baling contract?* I wondered.

It took me a few *days to understand* his question.
It took me several *years to appreciate* his question.

When I was a child, I heard the story of my grandfather's heart attack. He was not yet fifty at the time. Several years later, when I was a young adult, he gave me the details of that experience.

Granddad said that when he had the heart attack, he actually died. This was before people even dared speak of such things. "However," Granddad said, "I did die and go to the heavenly gates. Once there, I was met by the Lord, who told me that I was welcome to stay, but He did have more work for me to complete on the earth. He gave me the option of staying with Him in heaven, or going back to earth to fulfill what He wanted me to do. I told the Lord that I would go back, if that was His desire. I immediately opened my eyes and found myself in the hospital emergency room."

Granddad became a deacon in his church and a beacon to his community. To my knowledge, he never had another heart problem and kept his health until a few weeks before the Lord took him home. Yet his last thoughts and words were of his meeting with the Lord some forty years earlier. He had taken his assignment seriously. What an example.

I feel sure that my grandfather did complete his work on the earth. I only hope to complete mine in a similar manner. His sphere of influence was in a small country town in Texas. My sphere of influence is within the business community.

Where is your sphere of influence? Will you be diligent to complete your work and fulfill your destiny on this earth? I hope so. May God bless you in your efforts.

Endnotes

i. David High, *Kings and Priests* (Oklahoma City: Books for Children of the World, 1993).

ii. R. G. LeTourneau, *Mover of Men and Mountains* (Chicago: Moody Press, 1972), 79.

iii. *Ibid.*, 85.

iv. *Ibid.*

v. *Ibid.*, 103.

vi. Conrad Hilton, *Be My Guest* (New York: Fireside, 1994), 131.

vii. *Ibid.*, 23.

viii. *Ibid.*, 22.

ix. *Webster Illustrated Contemporary Dictionary Encyclopedia Edition*, s.v. "Steward."

x. *Webster Illustrated Contemporary Dictionary Encyclopedia Edition*, s.v. "Integrity."

xi. Randy Pennington and Marc Bockmon, *On My Honor, I Will* (New York: Warner Books, 1992), 155.

xii. *Webster Illustrated Contemporary Dictionary Encyclopedia Edition*, s.v. "Counsel."

xiii. David Yergin, *The Prize* (New York: Free Press, 1992), 47.

xiv. Max Lucado, *Grace for the Moment Morning & Evening Edition: Inspiration for Each Day of the Year* (Nashville: Thomas Nelson, 2008), 100.

ACKNOWLEDGMENTS

I would like to thank my wife, Shannon, for her support of this book. Your willingness to live with and support my business endeavors and growth as a Christian has meant everything to me. You have encouraged me to write this book just as you have always supported the many projects I have brought to our home. Thank you.

I also thank my children, Courtney and Matthew, for their feedback, editing skills, and moral support. All three members of my family have been very patient with me, as this book has been a very long-term project.

In addition, I thank all the friends, businesspeople, prayer partners, and ministers that have been a part of my spiritual and business growth, which served as the foundation for the concepts discussed in this book.

I especially thank the downtown (Tyler, Texas) Tuesday morning men's prayer group that read, discussed, and encouraged me with this project.

I must also make mention of the great help that the iUniverse editorial staff and Andrea Taylor's company, Third Chapter Press, provided with their editing skills, feedback, and final suggestions for the book. Thank you.

And finally, I would like to thank Charlotte Hale Pindar, my friend and editor. Charlotte, I thank you for your constant encouragement over the years. You helped me sort out my notes and get focused on this book. It was a great blessing to meet you ten years ago and become your friend!